Men, Women, and Ghosts

Men, Women, and Ghosts

Amy Lowell

MINT EDITIONS

Men, Women, and Ghosts was first published in 1916.

This edition published by Mint Editions 2021.

ISBN 9781513295879 | E-ISBN 9781513297378

Published by Mint Editions®

 MINT
EDITIONS

minteditionbooks.com

Publishing Director: Jennifer Newens
Design & Production: Rachel Lopez Metzger
Project Manager: Micaela Clark
Typesetting: Westchester Publishing Services

Contents

PREFACE

This is a book of stories. For that reason I have excluded all purely lyrical poems. But the word "stories" has been stretched to its fullest application. It includes both narrative poems, properly so called; tales divided into scenes; and a few pieces of less obvious story-telling import in which one might say that the dramatis personae are air, clouds, trees, houses, streets, and such like things.

It has long been a favourite idea of mine that the rhythms of 'vers libre' have not been sufficiently plumbed, that there is in them a power of variation which has never yet been brought to the light of experiment. I think it was the piano pieces of Debussy, with their strange likeness to short vers libre poems, which first showed me the close kinship of music and poetry, and there flashed into my mind the idea of using the movement of poetry in somewhat the same way that the musician uses the movement of music.

It was quite evident that this could never be done in the strict pattern of a metrical form, but the flowing, fluctuating rhythm of vers libre seemed to open the door to such an experiment. First, however, I considered the same method as applied to the more pronounced movements of natural objects. If the reader will turn to the poem, "A Roxbury Garden," he will find in the first two sections an attempt to give the circular movement of a hoop bowling along the ground, and the up and down, elliptical curve of a flying shuttlecock.

From these experiments, it is but a step to the flowing rhythm of music. In "The Cremona Violin," I have tried to give this flowing, changing rhythm to the parts in which the violin is being played. The effect is farther heightened, because the rest of the poem is written in the seven line Chaucerian stanza; and, by deserting this ordered pattern for the undulating line of vers libre, I hoped to produce something of the suave, continuous tone of a violin. Again, in the violin parts themselves, the movement constantly changes, as will be quite plain to any one reading these passages aloud.

In "The Cremona Violin," however, the rhythms are fairly obvious and regular. I set myself a far harder task in trying to transcribe the various movements of Stravinsky's "Three Pieces 'Grotesques', for String Quartet." Several musicians, who have seen the poem, think the movement accurately given.

These experiments lead me to believe that there is here much food for thought and matter for study, and I hope many poets will follow me in opening up the still hardly explored possibilities of vers libre.

A good many of the poems in this book are written in "polyphonic prose." A form about which I have written and spoken so much that it seems hardly necessary to explain it here. Let me hastily add, however, that the word "prose" in its name refers only to the typographical arrangement, for in no sense is this a prose form. Only read it aloud, Gentle Reader, I beg, and you will see what you will see. For a purely dramatic form, I know none better in the whole range of poetry. It enables the poet to give his characters the vivid, real effect they have in a play, while at the same time writing in the 'decor'.

One last innovation I have still to mention. It will be found in "Spring Day," and more fully enlarged upon in the series, "Towns in Colour." In these poems, I have endeavoured to give the colour, and light, and shade, of certain places and hours, stressing the purely pictorial effect, and with little or no reference to any other aspect of the places described. It is an enchanting thing to wander through a city looking for its unrelated beauty, the beauty by which it captivates the sensuous sense of seeing.

I have always loved aquariums, but for years I went to them and looked, and looked, at those swirling, shooting, looping patterns of fish, which always defied transcription to paper until I hit upon the "unrelated" method. The result is in "An Aquarium." I think the first thing which turned me in this direction was John Gould Fletcher's "London Excursion," in "Some Imagist Poets." I here record my thanks.

For the substance of the poems—why, the poems are here. No one writing today can fail to be affected by the great war raging in Europe at this time. We are too near it to do more than touch upon it. But, obliquely, it is suggested in many of these poems, most notably those in the section, "Bronze Tablets." The Napoleonic Era is an epic subject, and waits a great epic poet. I have only been able to open a few windows upon it here and there. But the scene from the windows is authentic, and the watcher has used eyes, and ears, and heart, in watching.

Amy Lowell
July 10, 1916

FIGURINES IN OLD SAXE

Patterns

I walk down the garden paths,
And all the daffodils
Are blowing, and the bright blue squills.
I walk down the patterned garden-paths
In my stiff, brocaded gown.
With my powdered hair and jewelled fan,
I too am a rare
Pattern. As I wander down
The garden paths.

My dress is richly figured,
And the train
Makes a pink and silver stain
On the gravel, and the thrift
Of the borders.
Just a plate of current fashion,
Tripping by in high-heeled, ribboned shoes.
Not a softness anywhere about me,
Only whalebone and brocade.
And I sink on a seat in the shade
Of a lime tree. For my passion
Wars against the stiff brocade.
The daffodils and squills
Flutter in the breeze
As they please.
And I weep;
For the lime-tree is in blossom
And one small flower has dropped upon my bosom.

And the plashing of waterdrops
In the marble fountain
Comes down the garden-paths.
The dripping never stops.
Underneath my stiffened gown
Is the softness of a woman bathing in a marble basin,
A basin in the midst of hedges grown

So thick, she cannot see her lover hiding,
But she guesses he is near,
And the sliding of the water
Seems the stroking of a dear
Hand upon her.
What is Summer in a fine brocaded gown!
I should like to see it lying in a heap upon the ground.
All the pink and silver crumpled up on the ground.

I would be the pink and silver as I ran along the paths,
And he would stumble after,
Bewildered by my laughter.
I should see the sun flashing from his sword-hilt and the buckles on
     his shoes.
I would choose
To lead him in a maze along the patterned paths,
A bright and laughing maze for my heavy-booted lover,
Till he caught me in the shade,
And the buttons of his waistcoat bruised my body as he clasped me,
Aching, melting, unafraid.
With the shadows of the leaves and the sundrops,
And the plopping of the waterdrops,
All about us in the open afternoon—
I am very like to swoon
With the weight of this brocade,
For the sun sifts through the shade.

Underneath the fallen blossom
In my bosom,
Is a letter I have hid.
It was brought to me this morning by a rider from the Duke.
"Madam, we regret to inform you that Lord Hartwell
 Died in action Thursday se'nnight."
As I read it in the white, morning sunlight,
 The letters squirmed like snakes.
"Any answer, Madam," said my footman.
"No," I told him.
"See that the messenger takes some refreshment.
 No, no answer."

And I walked into the garden,
Up and down the patterned paths,
In my stiff, correct brocade.
The blue and yellow flowers stood up proudly in the sun,
Each one.
I stood upright too,
Held rigid to the pattern
By the stiffness of my gown.
Up and down I walked,
Up and down.

In a month he would have been my husband.
In a month, here, underneath this lime,
We would have broke the pattern;
He for me, and I for him,
He as Colonel, I as Lady,
On this shady seat.
He had a whim
That sunlight carried blessing.
And I answered, "It shall be as you have said."
Now he is dead.

In Summer and in Winter I shall walk
Up and down
The patterned garden-paths
In my stiff, brocaded gown.
The squills and daffodils
Will give place to pillared roses, and to asters, and to snow.
I shall go
Up and down,
In my gown.
Gorgeously arrayed,
Boned and stayed.
And the softness of my body will be guarded from embrace
By each button, hook, and lace.
For the man who should loose me is dead,
Fighting with the Duke in Flanders,
In a pattern called a war.
Christ! What are patterns for?

PICKTHORN MANOR

I

How fresh the Dartle's little waves that day!
    A steely silver, underlined with blue,
And flashing where the round clouds, blown away,
    Let drop the yellow sunshine to gleam through
And tip the edges of the waves with shifts
    And spots of whitest fire, hard like gems
        Cut from the midnight moon they were, and sharp
    As wind through leafless stems.
The Lady Eunice walked between the drifts
Of blooming cherry-trees, and watched the rifts
        Of clouds drawn through the river's azure warp.

II

Her little feet tapped softly down the path.
    Her soul was listless; even the morning breeze
Fluttering the trees and strewing a light swath
    Of fallen petals on the grass, could please
Her not at all. She brushed a hair aside
    With a swift move, and a half-angry frown.
        She stopped to pull a daffodil or two,
    And held them to her gown
To test the colours; put them at her side,
Then at her breast, then loosened them and tried
        Some new arrangement, but it would not do.

III

A lady in a Manor-house, alone,
    Whose husband is in Flanders with the Duke
Of Marlborough and Prince Eugene, she's grown
    Too apathetic even to rebuke
Her idleness. What is she on this Earth?
    No woman surely, since she neither can

Be wed nor single, must not let her mind
    Build thoughts upon a man
Except for hers. Indeed that were no dearth
Were her Lord here, for well she knew his worth,
        And when she thought of him her eyes were kind.

IV

Too lately wed to have forgot the wooing.
    Too unaccustomed as a bride to feel
Other than strange delight at her wife's doing.
    Even at the thought a gentle blush would steal
Over her face, and then her lips would frame
    Some little word of loving, and her eyes
        Would brim and spill their tears, when all they saw
    Was the bright sun, slantwise
Through burgeoning trees, and all the morning's flame
Burning and quivering round her. With quick shame
        She shut her heart and bent before the law.

V

He was a soldier, she was proud of that.
    This was his house and she would keep it well.
His honour was in fighting, hers in what
    He'd left her here in charge of. Then a spell
Of conscience sent her through the orchard spying
    Upon the gardeners. Were their tools about?
        Were any branches broken? Had the weeds
    Been duly taken out
Under the 'spaliered pears, and were these lying
Nailed snug against the sunny bricks and drying
        Their leaves and satisfying all their needs?

VI

She picked a stone up with a little pout,
    Stones looked so ill in well-kept flower-borders.
Where should she put it? All the paths about
    Were strewn with fair, red gravel by her orders.
No stone could mar their sifted smoothness. So
    She hurried to the river. At the edge
        She stood a moment charmed by the swift blue
    Beyond the river sedge.
She watched it curdling, crinkling, and the snow
Purfled upon its wave-tops. Then, "Hullo,
        My Beauty, gently, or you'll wriggle through."

VII

The Lady Eunice caught a willow spray
    To save herself from tumbling in the shallows
Which rippled to her feet. Then straight away
    She peered down stream among the budding sallows.
A youth in leather breeches and a shirt
    Of finest broidered lawn lay out upon
        An overhanging bole and deftly swayed
    A well-hooked fish which shone
In the pale lemon sunshine like a spurt
Of silver, bowed and damascened, and girt
        With crimson spots and moons which waned and played.

VIII

The fish hung circled for a moment, ringed
    And bright; then flung itself out, a thin blade
Of spotted lightning, and its tail was winged
    With chipped and sparkled sunshine. And the shade
Broke up and splintered into shafts of light
    Wheeling about the fish, who churned the air
        And made the fish-line hum, and bent the rod
    Almost to snapping. Care
The young man took against the twigs, with slight,

Deft movements he kept fish and line in tight
    Obedience to his will with every prod.

IX

He lay there, and the fish hung just beyond.
    He seemed uncertain what more he should do.
He drew back, pulled the rod to correspond,
    Tossed it and caught it; every time he threw,
He caught it nearer to the point. At last
    The fish was near enough to touch. He paused.
        Eunice knew well the craft—"What's got the thing!"
    She cried. "What can have caused—
Where is his net? The moment will be past.
The fish will wriggle free." She stopped aghast.
        He turned and bowed. One arm was in a sling.

X

The broad, black ribbon she had thought his basket
    Must hang from, held instead a useless arm.
"I do not wonder, Madam, that you ask it."
    He smiled, for she had spoke aloud. "The charm
Of trout fishing is in my eyes enhanced
    When you must play your fish on land as well."
        "How will you take him?" Eunice asked. "In truth
    I really cannot tell.
'Twas stupid of me, but it simply chanced
I never thought of that until he glanced
        Into the branches. 'Tis a bit uncouth."

XI

He watched the fish against the blowing sky,
    Writhing and glittering, pulling at the line.
"The hook is fast, I might just let him die,"
    He mused. "But that would jar against your fine
Sense of true sportsmanship, I know it would,"
    Cried Eunice. "Let me do it." Swift and light

She ran towards him. "It is so long now
    Since I have felt a bite,
I lost all heart for everything." She stood,
Supple and strong, beside him, and her blood
    Tingled her lissom body to a glow.

XII

She quickly seized the fish and with a stone
    Ended its flurry, then removed the hook,
Untied the fly with well-poised fingers. Done,
    She asked him where he kept his fishing-book.
He pointed to a coat flung on the ground.
    She searched the pockets, found a shagreen case,
        Replaced the fly, noticed a golden stamp
    Filling the middle space.
Two letters half rubbed out were there, and round
About them gay rococo flowers wound
        And tossed a spray of roses to the clamp.

XIII

The Lady Eunice puzzled over these.
    "G. D." the young man gravely said. "My name
Is Gervase Deane. Your servant, if you please."
    "Oh, Sir, indeed I know you, for your fame
For exploits in the field has reached my ears.
    I did not know you wounded and returned."
        "But just come back, Madam. A silly prick
    To gain me such unearned
Holiday making. And you, it appears,
Must be Sir Everard's lady. And my fears
        At being caught a-trespassing were quick."

XIV

He looked so rueful that she laughed out loud.
    "You are forgiven, Mr. Deane. Even more,
I offer you the fishing, and am proud

That you should find it pleasant from this shore.
Nobody fishes now, my husband used
    To angle daily, and I too with him.
        He loved the spotted trout, and pike, and dace.
    He even had a whim
That flies my fingers tied swiftly confused
The greater fish. And he must be excused,
        Love weaves odd fancies in a lonely place."

XV

She sighed because it seemed so long ago,
    Those days with Everard; unthinking took
The path back to the orchard. Strolling so
    She walked, and he beside her. In a nook
Where a stone seat withdrew beneath low boughs,
    Full-blossomed, hummed with bees, they sat them down.
        She questioned him about the war, the share
    Her husband had, and grown
Eager by his clear answers, straight allows
Her hidden hopes and fears to speak, and rouse
        Her numbed love, which had slumbered unaware.

XVI

Under the orchard trees daffodils danced
    And jostled, turning sideways to the wind.
A dropping cherry petal softly glanced
    Over her hair, and slid away behind.
At the far end through twisted cherry-trees
    The old house glowed, geranium-hued, with bricks
        Bloomed in the sun like roses, low and long,
    Gabled, and with quaint tricks
Of chimneys carved and fretted. Out of these
Grey smoke was shaken, which the faint Spring breeze
        Tossed into nothing. Then a thrush's song

XVII

Needled its way through sound of bees and river.
    The notes fell, round and starred, between young leaves,
Trilled to a spiral lilt, stopped on a quiver.
    The Lady Eunice listens and believes.
Gervase has many tales of her dear Lord,
    His bravery, his knowledge, his charmed life.
        She quite forgets who's speaking in the gladness
    Of being this man's wife.
Gervase is wounded, grave indeed, the word
Is kindly said, but to a softer chord
        She strings her voice to ask with wistful sadness,

XVIII

"And is Sir Everard still unscathed? I fain
    Would know the truth." "Quite well, dear Lady, quite."
She smiled in her content. "So many slain,
    You must forgive me for a little fright."
And he forgave her, not alone for that,
    But because she was fingering his heart,
        Pressing and squeezing it, and thinking so
    Only to ease her smart
Of painful, apprehensive longing. At
Their feet the river swirled and chucked. They sat
        An hour there. The thrush flew to and fro.

XIX

The Lady Eunice supped alone that day,
    As always since Sir Everard had gone,
In the oak-panelled parlour, whose array
    Of faded portraits in carved mouldings shone.
Warriors and ladies, armoured, ruffed, peruked.
    Van Dykes with long, slim fingers; Holbeins, stout
        And heavy-featured; and one Rubens dame,
    A peony just burst out,
With flaunting, crimson flesh. Eunice rebuked

Her thoughts of gentler blood, when these had duked
      It with the best, and scorned to change their name.

XX

A sturdy family, and old besides,
    Much older than her own, the Earls of Crowe.
Since Saxon days, these men had sought their brides
    Among the highest born, but always so,
Taking them to themselves, their wealth, their lands,
    But never their titles. Stern perhaps, but strong,
        The Framptons fed their blood from richest streams,
    Scorning the common throng.
Gazing upon these men, she understands
The toughness of the web wrought from such strands
      And pride of Everard colours all her dreams.

XXI

Eunice forgets to eat, watching their faces
    Flickering in the wind-blown candle's shine.
Blue-coated lackeys tiptoe to their places,
    And set out plates of fruit and jugs of wine.
The table glitters black like Winter ice.
    The Dartle's rushing, and the gentle clash
        Of blossomed branches, drifts into her ears.
    And through the casement sash
She sees each cherry stem a pointed slice
Of splintered moonlight, topped with all the spice
      And shimmer of the blossoms it uprears.

XXII

"In such a night—" she laid the book aside,
    She could outnight the poet by thinking back.
In such a night she came here as a bride.
    The date was graven in the almanack
Of her clasped memory. In this very room
    Had Everard uncloaked her. On this seat

Had drawn her to him, bade her note the trees,
 How white they were and sweet
And later, coming to her, her dear groom,
Her Lord, had lain beside her in the gloom
 Of moon and shade, and whispered her to ease.

XXIII

Her little taper made the room seem vast,
 Caverned and empty. And her beating heart
Rapped through the silence all about her cast
 Like some loud, dreadful death-watch taking part
In this sad vigil. Slowly she undrest,
 Put out the light and crept into her bed.
 The linen sheets were fragrant, but so cold.
 And brimming tears she shed,
Sobbing and quivering in her barren nest,
Her weeping lips into the pillow prest,
 Her eyes sealed fast within its smothering fold.

XXIV

The morning brought her a more stoic mind,
 And sunshine struck across the polished floor.
She wondered whether this day she should find
 Gervase a-fishing, and so listen more,
Much more again, to all he had to tell.
 And he was there, but waiting to begin
 Until she came. They fished awhile, then went
 To the old seat within
The cherry's shade. He pleased her very well
By his discourse. But ever he must dwell
 Upon Sir Everard. Each incident

XXV

Must be related and each term explained.
 How troops were set in battle, how a siege
Was ordered and conducted. She complained

Because he bungled at the fall of Liege.
The curious names of parts of forts she knew,
    And aired with conscious pride her ravelins,
        And counterscarps, and lunes. The day drew on,
    And his dead fish's fins
In the hot sunshine turned a mauve-green hue.
At last Gervase, guessing the hour, withdrew.
        But she sat long in still oblivion.

XXVI

Then he would bring her books, and read to her
    The poems of Dr. Donne, and the blue river
Would murmur through the reading, and a stir
    Of birds and bees make the white petals shiver,
And one or two would flutter prone and lie
    Spotting the smooth-clipped grass. The days went by
        Threaded with talk and verses. Green leaves pushed
    Through blossoms stubbornly.
Gervase, unconscious of dishonesty,
Fell into strong and watchful loving, free
        He thought, since always would his lips be hushed.

XXVII

But lips do not stay silent at command,
    And Gervase strove in vain to order his.
Luckily Eunice did not understand
    That he but read himself aloud, for this
Their friendship would have snapped. She treated him
    And spoilt him like a brother. It was now
        "Gervase" and "Eunice" with them, and he dined
    Whenever she'd allow,
In the oak parlour, underneath the dim
Old pictured Framptons, opposite her slim
        Figure, so bright against the chair behind.

XXVIII

Eunice was happier than she had been
    For many days, and yet the hours were long.
All Gervase told to her but made her lean
    More heavily upon the past. Among
Her hopes she lived, even when she was giving
    Her morning orders, even when she twined
        Nosegays to deck her parlours. With the thought
    Of Everard, her mind
Solaced its solitude, and in her striving
To do as he would wish was all her living.
        She welcomed Gervase for the news he brought.

XXIX

Black-hearts and white-hearts, bubbled with the sun,
    Hid in their leaves and knocked against each other.
Eunice was standing, panting with her run
    Up to the tool-house just to get another
Basket. All those which she had brought were filled,
    And still Gervase pelted her from above.
        The buckles of his shoes flashed higher and higher
    Until his shoulders strove
Quite through the top. "Eunice, your spirit's filled
This tree. White-hearts!" He shook, and cherries spilled
        And spat out from the leaves like falling fire.

XXX

The wide, sun-winged June morning spread itself
    Over the quiet garden. And they packed
Full twenty baskets with the fruit. "My shelf
    Of cordials will be stored with what it lacked.
In future, none of us will drink strong ale,
    But cherry-brandy." "Vastly good, I vow,"
        And Gervase gave the tree another shake.
    The cherries seemed to flow
Out of the sky in cloudfuls, like blown hail.

Swift Lady Eunice ran, her farthingale,
      Unnoticed, tangling in a fallen rake.

XXXI

She gave a little cry and fell quite prone
      In the long grass, and lay there very still.
Gervase leapt from the tree at her soft moan,
      And kneeling over her, with clumsy skill
Unloosed her bodice, fanned her with his hat,
      And his unguarded lips pronounced his heart.
         "Eunice, my Dearest Girl, where are you hurt?"
      His trembling fingers dart
Over her limbs seeking some wound. She strove
To answer, opened wide her eyes, above
      Her knelt Sir Everard, with face alert.

XXXII

Her eyelids fell again at that sweet sight,
      "My Love!" she murmured, "Dearest! Oh, my Dear!"
He took her in his arms and bore her right
      And tenderly to the old seat, and "Here
I have you mine at last," she said, and swooned
      Under his kisses. When she came once more
         To sight of him, she smiled in comfort knowing
      Herself laid as before
Close covered on his breast. And all her glowing
Youth answered him, and ever nearer growing
      She twined him in her arms and soft festooned

XXXIII

Herself about him like a flowering vine,
      Drawing his lips to cling upon her own.
A ray of sunlight pierced the leaves to shine
      Where her half-opened bodice let be shown
Her white throat fluttering to his soft caress,
      Half-gasping with her gladness. And her pledge

She whispers, melting with delight. A twig
　　Snaps in the hornbeam hedge.
A cackling laugh tears through the quietness.
Eunice starts up in terrible distress.
　　　"My God! What's that?" Her staring eyes are big.

XXXIV

Revulsed emotion set her body shaking
　　As though she had an ague. Gervase swore,
Jumped to his feet in such a dreadful taking
　　His face was ghastly with the look it wore.
Crouching and slipping through the trees, a man
　　In worn, blue livery, a humpbacked thing,
　　　　Made off. But turned every few steps to gaze
　　At Eunice, and to fling
Vile looks and gestures back. "The ruffian!
By Christ's Death! I will split him to a span
　　　　Of hog's thongs." She grasped at his sleeve, "Gervase!

XXXV

What are you doing here? Put down that sword,
　　That's only poor old Tony, crazed and lame.
We never notice him. With my dear Lord
　　I ought not to have minded that he came.
But, Gervase, it surprises me that you
　　Should so lack grace to stay here." With one hand
　　　　She held her gaping bodice to conceal
　　Her breast. "I must demand
Your instant absence. Everard, but new
Returned, will hardly care for guests. Adieu."
　　　　"Eunice, you're mad." His brain began to reel.

XXXVI

He tried again to take her, tried to twist
　　Her arms about him. Truly, she had said
Nothing should ever part them. In a mist

　　　　　　　　　　　　　　　　　　　　AMY LOWELL

She pushed him from her, clasped her aching head
In both her hands, and rocked and sobbed aloud.
   "Oh! Where is Everard? What does this mean?
      So lately come to leave me thus alone!"
   But Gervase had not seen
Sir Everard. Then, gently, to her bowed
And sickening spirit, he told of her proud
      Surrender to him. He could hear her moan.

XXXVII

Then shame swept over her and held her numb,
   Hiding her anguished face against the seat.
At last she rose, a woman stricken—dumb—
   And trailed away with slowly-dragging feet.
Gervase looked after her, but feared to pass
   The barrier set between them. All his rare
      Joy broke to fragments—worse than that, unreal.
   And standing lonely there,
His swollen heart burst out, and on the grass
He flung himself and wept. He knew, alas!
      The loss so great his life could never heal.

XXXVIII

For days thereafter Eunice lived retired,
   Waited upon by one old serving-maid.
She would not leave her chamber, and desired
   Only to hide herself. She was afraid
Of what her eyes might trick her into seeing,
   Of what her longing urge her then to do.
      What was this dreadful illness solitude
   Had tortured her into?
Her hours went by in a long constant fleeing
The thought of that one morning. And her being
      Bruised itself on a happening so rude.

XXXIX

It grew ripe Summer, when one morning came
    Her tirewoman with a letter, printed
Upon the seal were the Deane crest and name.
    With utmost gentleness, the letter hinted
His understanding and his deep regret.
    But would she not permit him once again
        To pay her his profound respects? No word
    Of what had passed should pain
Her resolution. Only let them get
Back the old comradeship. Her eyes were wet
        With starting tears, now truly she deplored

XL

His misery. Yes, she was wrong to keep
    Away from him. He hardly was to blame.
'Twas she—she shuddered and began to weep.
    'Twas her fault! Hers! Her everlasting shame
Was that she suffered him, whom not at all
    She loved. Poor Boy! Yes, they must still be friends.
        She owed him that to keep the balance straight.
    It was such poor amends
Which she could make for rousing hopes to gall
Him with their unfulfilment. Tragical
        It was, and she must leave him desolate.

XLI

Hard silence he had forced upon his lips
    For long and long, and would have done so still
Had not she—here she pressed her finger tips
    Against her heavy eyes. Then with forced will
She wrote that he might come, sealed with the arms
    Of Crowe and Frampton twined. Her heart felt lighter
        When this was done. It seemed her constant care
    Might some day cease to fright her.
Illness could be no crime, and dreadful harms

                                           AMY LOWELL

Did come from too much sunshine. Her alarms
        Would lessen when she saw him standing there,

XLII

Simple and kind, a brother just returned
        From journeying, and he would treat her so.
She knew his honest heart, and if there burned
        A spark in it he would not let it show.
But when he really came, and stood beside
        Her underneath the fruitless cherry boughs,
            He seemed a tired man, gaunt, leaden-eyed.
        He made her no more vows,
Nor did he mention one thing he had tried
To put into his letter. War supplied
        Him topics. And his mind seemed occupied.

XLIII

Daily they met. And gravely walked and talked.
        He read her no more verses, and he stayed
Only until their conversation, balked
        Of every natural channel, fled dismayed.
Again the next day she would meet him, trying
        To give her tone some healthy sprightliness,
            But his uneager dignity soon chilled
        Her well-prepared address.
Thus Summer waned, and in the mornings, crying
Of wild geese startled Eunice, and their flying
        Whirred overhead for days and never stilled.

XLIV

One afternoon of grey clouds and white wind,
        Eunice awaited Gervase by the river.
The Dartle splashed among the reeds and whined
        Over the willow-roots, and a long sliver
Of caked and slobbered foam crept up the bank.
        All through the garden, drifts of skirling leaves

Blew up, and settled down, and blew again.
The cherry-trees were weaves
Of empty, knotted branches, and a dank
Mist hid the house, mouldy it smelt and rank
With sodden wood, and still unfalling rain.

XLV

Eunice paced up and down. No joy she took
At meeting Gervase, but the custom grown
Still held her. He was late. She sudden shook,
And caught at her stopped heart. Her eyes had shown
Sir Everard emerging from the mist.
His uniform was travel-stained and torn,
His jackboots muddy, and his eager stride
Jangled his spurs. A thorn
Entangled, trailed behind him. To the tryst
He hastened. Eunice shuddered, ran—a twist
Round a sharp turning and she fled to hide.

XLVI

But he had seen her as she swiftly ran,
A flash of white against the river's grey.
"Eunice," he called. "My Darling. Eunice. Can
You hear me? It is Everard. All day
I have been riding like the very devil
To reach you sooner. Are you startled, Dear?"
He broke into a run and followed her,
And caught her, faint with fear,
Cowering and trembling as though she some evil
Spirit were seeing. "What means this uncivil
Greeting, Dear Heart?" He saw her senses blur.

XLVII

Swaying and catching at the seat, she tried
To speak, but only gurgled in her throat.
At last, straining to hold herself, she cried

To him for pity, and her strange words smote
A coldness through him, for she begged Gervase
    To leave her, 'twas too much a second time.
        Gervase must go, always Gervase, her mind
    Repeated like a rhyme
This name he did not know. In sad amaze
He watched her, and that hunted, fearful gaze,
        So unremembering and so unkind.

XLVIII

Softly he spoke to her, patiently dealt
    With what he feared her madness. By and by
He pierced her understanding. Then he knelt
    Upon the seat, and took her hands: "Now try
To think a minute I am come, my Dear,
    Unharmed and back on furlough. Are you glad
        To have your lover home again? To me,
    Pickthorn has never had
A greater pleasantness. Could you not bear
To come and sit awhile beside me here?
        A stone between us surely should not be."

XLIX

She smiled a little wan and ravelled smile,
    Then came to him and on his shoulder laid
Her head, and they two rested there awhile,
    Each taking comfort. Not a word was said.
But when he put his hand upon her breast
    And felt her beating heart, and with his lips
        Sought solace for her and himself. She started
    As one sharp lashed with whips,
And pushed him from her, moaning, his dumb quest
Denied and shuddered from. And he, distrest,
        Loosened his wife, and long they sat there, parted.

L

Eunice was very quiet all that day,
 A little dazed, and yet she seemed content.
At candle-time, he asked if she would play
 Upon her harpsichord, at once she went
And tinkled airs from Lully's 'Carnival'
 And 'Bacchus', newly brought away from France.
 Then jaunted through a lively rigadoon
 To please him with a dance
By Purcell, for he said that surely all
Good Englishmen had pride in national
 Accomplishment. But tiring of it soon

LI

He whispered her that if she had forgiven
 His startling her that afternoon, the clock
Marked early bed-time. Surely it was Heaven
 He entered when she opened to his knock.
The hours rustled in the trailing wind
 Over the chimney. Close they lay and knew
 Only that they were wedded. At his touch
 Anxiety she threw
Away like a shed garment, and inclined
Herself to cherish him, her happy mind
 Quivering, unthinking, loving overmuch.

LII

Eunice lay long awake in the cool night
 After her husband slept. She gazed with joy
Into the shadows, painting them with bright
 Pictures of all her future life's employ.
Twin gems they were, set to a single jewel,
 Each shining with the other. Soft she turned
 And felt his breath upon her hair, and prayed
 Her happiness was earned.
Past Earls of Crowe should give their blood for fuel

To light this Frampton's hearth-fire. By no cruel
  Affrightings would she ever be dismayed.

LIII

When Everard, next day, asked her in joke
  What name it was that she had called him by,
She told him of Gervase, and as she spoke
  She hardly realized it was a lie.
Her vision she related, but she hid
  The fondness into which she had been led.
    Sir Everard just laughed and pinched her ear,
  And quite out of her head
The matter drifted. Then Sir Everard chid
Himself for laziness, and off he rid
    To see his men and count his farming-gear.

LIV

At supper he seemed overspread with gloom,
  But gave no reason why, he only asked
More questions of Gervase, and round the room
  He walked with restless strides. At last he tasked
Her with a greater feeling for this man
  Than she had given. Eunice quick denied
    The slightest interest other than a friend
  Might claim. But he replied
He thought she underrated. Then a ban
He put on talk and music. He'd a plan
    To work at, draining swamps at Pickthorn End.

LV

Next morning Eunice found her Lord still changed,
  Hard and unkind, with bursts of anger. Pride
Kept him from speaking out. His probings ranged
  All round his torment. Lady Eunice tried
To sooth him. So a week went by, and then
  His anguish flooded over; with clenched hands

Striving to stem his words, he told her plain
    Tony had seen them, "brands
Burning in Hell," the man had said. Again
Eunice described her vision, and how when
        Awoke at last she had known dreadful pain.

LVI

He could not credit it, and misery fed
    Upon his spirit, day by day it grew.
To Gervase he forbade the house, and led
    The Lady Eunice such a life she flew
At his approaching footsteps. Winter came
        Snowing and blustering through the Manor trees.
            All the roof-edges spiked with icicles
        In fluted companies.
The Lady Eunice with her tambour-frame
Kept herself sighing company. The flame
        Of the birch fire glittered on the walls.

LVII

A letter was brought to her as she sat,
    Unsealed, unsigned. It told her that his wound,
The writer's, had so well recovered that
    To join his regiment he felt him bound.
But would she not wish him one short "Godspeed,"
    He asked no more. Her greeting would suffice.
        He had resolved he never should return.
    Would she this sacrifice
Make for a dying man? How could she read
The rest! But forcing her eyes to the deed,
        She read. Then dropped it in the fire to burn.

LVIII

Gervase had set the river for their meeting
    As farthest from the farms where Everard
Spent all his days. How should he know such cheating

Was quite expected, at least no dullard
Was Everard Frampton. Hours by hours he hid
    Among the willows watching. Dusk had come,
        And from the Manor he had long been gone.
    Eunice her burdensome
Task set about. Hooded and cloaked, she slid
Over the slippery paths, and soon amid
        The sallows saw a boat tied to a stone.

LIX

Gervase arose, and kissed her hand, then pointed
    Into the boat. She shook her head, but he
Begged her to realize why, and with disjointed
    Words told her of what peril there might be
From listeners along the river bank.
    A push would take them out of earshot. Ten
        Minutes was all he asked, then she should land,
    He go away again,
Forever this time. Yet how could he thank
Her for so much compassion. Here she sank
        Upon a thwart, and bid him quick unstrand

LX

His boat. He cast the rope, and shoved the keel
    Free of the gravel; jumped, and dropped beside
Her; took the oars, and they began to steal
    Under the overhanging trees. A wide
Gash of red lantern-light cleft like a blade
    Into the gloom, and struck on Eunice sitting
        Rigid and stark upon the after thwart.
    It blazed upon their flitting
In merciless light. A moment so it stayed,
Then was extinguished, and Sir Everard made
        One leap, and landed just a fraction short.

LXI

His weight upon the gunwale tipped the boat
    To straining balance. Everard lurched and seized
His wife and held her smothered to his coat.
    "Everard, loose me, we shall drown—" and squeezed
Against him, she beat with her hands. He gasped
    "Never, by God!" The slidden boat gave way
        And the black foamy water split—and met.
    Bubbled up through the spray
A wailing rose and in the branches rasped,
And creaked, and stilled. Over the treetops, clasped
        In the blue evening, a clear moon was set.

LXII

They lie entangled in the twisting roots,
    Embraced forever. Their cold marriage bed
Close-canopied and curtained by the shoots
    Of willows and pale birches. At the head,
White lilies, like still swans, placidly float
    And sway above the pebbles. Here are waves
        Sun-smitten for a threaded counterpane
    Gold-woven on their graves.
In perfect quietness they sleep, remote
In the green, rippled twilight. Death has smote
        Them to perpetual oneness who were twain.

AMY LOWELL

The Cremona Violin

Part First

Frau Concert-Meister Altgelt shut the door.
A storm was rising, heavy gusts of wind
Swirled through the trees, and scattered leaves before
Her on the clean, flagged path. The sky behind
The distant town was black, and sharp defined
Against it shone the lines of roofs and towers,
Superimposed and flat like cardboard flowers.

A pasted city on a purple ground,
Picked out with luminous paint, it seemed. The cloud
Split on an edge of lightning, and a sound
Of rivers full and rushing boomed through bowed,
Tossed, hissing branches. Thunder rumbled loud
Beyond the town fast swallowing into gloom.
Frau Altgelt closed the windows of each room.

She bustled round to shake by constant moving
The strange, weird atmosphere. She stirred the fire,
She twitched the supper-cloth as though improving
Its careful setting, then her own attire
Came in for notice, tiptoeing higher and higher
She peered into the wall-glass, now adjusting
A straying lock, or else a ribbon thrusting

This way or that to suit her. At last sitting,
Or rather plumping down upon a chair,
She took her work, the stocking she was knitting,
And watched the rain upon the window glare
In white, bright drops. Through the black glass a flare
Of lightning squirmed about her needles. "Oh!"
She cried. "What can be keeping Theodore so!"

A roll of thunder set the casements clapping.
Frau Altgelt flung her work aside and ran,
Pulled open the house door, with kerchief flapping
She stood and gazed along the street. A man
Flung back the garden-gate and nearly ran
Her down as she stood in the door. "Why, Dear,
What in the name of patience brings you here?

Quick, Lotta, shut the door, my violin
I fear is wetted. Now, Dear, bring a light.
This clasp is very much too worn and thin.
I'll take the other fiddle out tonight
If it still rains. Tut! Tut! my child, you're quite
Clumsy. Here, help me, hold the case while I—
Give me the candle. No, the inside's dry.

Thank God for that! Well, Lotta, how are you?
A bad storm, but the house still stands, I see.
Is my pipe filled, my Dear? I'll have a few
Puffs and a snooze before I eat my tea.
What do you say? That you were feared for me?
Nonsense, my child. Yes, kiss me, now don't talk.
I need a rest, the theatre's a long walk."

Her needles still, her hands upon her lap
Patiently laid, Charlotta Altgelt sat
And watched the rain-run window. In his nap
Her husband stirred and muttered. Seeing that,
Charlotta rose and softly, pit-a-pat,
Climbed up the stairs, and in her little room
Found sighing comfort with a moon in bloom.

But even rainy windows, silver-lit
By a new-burst, storm-whetted moon, may give
But poor content to loneliness, and it
Was hard for young Charlotta so to strive
And down her eagerness and learn to live
In placid quiet. While her husband slept,
Charlotta in her upper chamber wept.

AMY LOWELL

Herr Concert-Meister Altgelt was a man
Gentle and unambitious, that alone
Had kept him back. He played as few men can,
Drawing out of his instrument a tone
So shimmering-sweet and palpitant, it shone
Like a bright thread of sound hung in the air,
Afloat and swinging upward, slim and fair.

Above all things, above Charlotta his wife,
Herr Altgelt loved his violin, a fine
Cremona pattern, Stradivari's life
Was flowering out of early discipline
When this was fashioned. Of soft-cutting pine
The belly was. The back of broadly curled
Maple, the head made thick and sharply whirled.

The slanting, youthful sound-holes through
The belly of fine, vigorous pine
Mellowed each note and blew
It out again with a woody flavour
Tanged and fragrant as fir-trees are
When breezes in their needles jar.

The varnish was an orange-brown
Lustered like glass that's long laid down
Under a crumbling villa stone.
Purfled stoutly, with mitres which point
Straight up the corners. Each curve and joint
Clear, and bold, and thin.
Such was Herr Theodore's violin.

Seven o'clock, the Concert-Meister gone
With his best violin, the rain being stopped,
Frau Lotta in the kitchen sat alone
Watching the embers which the fire dropped.
The china shone upon the dresser, topped
By polished copper vessels which her skill
Kept brightly burnished. It was very still.

An air from 'Orfeo' hummed in her head.
Herr Altgelt had been practising before
The night's performance. Charlotta had plead
With him to stay with her. Even at the door
She'd begged him not to go. "I do implore
You for this evening, Theodore," she had said.
"Leave them tonight, and stay with me instead."

"A silly poppet!" Theodore pinched her ear.
"You'd like to have our good Elector turn
Me out I think." "But, Theodore, something queer
Ails me. Oh, do but notice how they burn,
My cheeks! The thunder worried me. You're stern,
And cold, and only love your work, I know.
But Theodore, for this evening, do not go."

But he had gone, hurriedly at the end,
For she had kept him talking. Now she sat
Alone again, always alone, the trend
Of all her thinking brought her back to that
She wished to banish. What would life be? What?
For she was young, and loved, while he was moved
Only by music. Each day that was proved.

Each day he rose and practised. While he played,
She stopped her work and listened, and her heart
Swelled painfully beneath her bodice. Swayed
And longing, she would hide from him her smart.
"Well, Lottchen, will that do?" Then what a start
She gave, and she would run to him and cry,
And he would gently chide her, "Fie, Dear, fie.

I'm glad I played it well. But such a taking!
You'll hear the thing enough before I've done."
And she would draw away from him, still shaking.
Had he but guessed she was another one,
Another violin. Her strings were aching,
Stretched to the touch of his bow hand, again
He played and she almost broke at the strain.

Where was the use of thinking of it now,
Sitting alone and listening to the clock!
She'd best make haste and knit another row.
Three hours at least must pass before his knock
Would startle her. It always was a shock.
She listened—listened—for so long before,
That when it came her hearing almost tore.

She caught herself just starting in to listen.
What nerves she had: rattling like brittle sticks!
She wandered to the window, for the glisten
Of a bright moon was tempting. Snuffed the wicks
Of her two candles. Still she could not fix
To anything. The moon in a broad swath
Beckoned her out and down the garden-path.

Against the house, her hollyhocks stood high
And black, their shadows doubling them. The night
Was white and still with moonlight, and a sigh
Of blowing leaves was there, and the dim flight
Of insects, and the smell of aconite,
And stocks, and Marvel of Peru. She flitted
Along the path, where blocks of shadow pitted

The even flags. She let herself go dreaming
Of Theodore her husband, and the tune
From 'Orfeo' swam through her mind, but seeming
Changed—shriller. Of a sudden, the clear moon
Showed her a passer-by, inopportune
Indeed, but here he was, whistling and striding.
Lotta squeezed in between the currants, hiding.

"The best laid plans of mice and men," alas!
The stranger came indeed, but did not pass.
Instead, he leant upon the garden-gate,
Folding his arms and whistling. Lotta's state,
Crouched in the prickly currants, on wet grass,
Was far from pleasant. Still the stranger stayed,
And Lotta in her currants watched, dismayed.

He seemed a proper fellow standing there
In the bright moonshine. His cocked hat was laced
With silver, and he wore his own brown hair
Tied, but unpowdered. His whole bearing graced
A fine cloth coat, and ruffled shirt, and chased
Sword-hilt. Charlotta looked, but her position
Was hardly easy. When would his volition

Suggest his walking on? And then that tune!
A half-a-dozen bars from 'Orfeo'
Gone over and over, and murdered. What Fortune
Had brought him there to stare about him so?
"Ach, Gott im Himmel! Why will he not go!"
Thought Lotta, but the young man whistled on,
And seemed in no great hurry to be gone.

Charlotta, crouched among the currant bushes,
Watched the moon slowly dip from twig to twig.
If Theodore should chance to come, and blushes
Streamed over her. He would not care a fig,
He'd only laugh. She pushed aside a sprig
Of sharp-edged leaves and peered, then she uprose
Amid her bushes. "Sir," said she, "pray whose

Garden do you suppose you're watching? Why
Do you stand there? I really must insist
Upon your leaving. 'Tis unmannerly
To stay so long." The young man gave a twist
And turned about, and in the amethyst
Moonlight he saw her like a nymph half-risen
From the green bushes which had been her prison.

He swept his hat off in a hurried bow.
"Your pardon, Madam, I had no idea
I was not quite alone, and that is how
I came to stay. My trespass was not sheer
Impertinence. I thought no one was here,
And really gardens cry to be admired.
Tonight especially it seemed required.

And may I beg to introduce myself?
Heinrich Marohl of Munich. And your name?"
Charlotta told him. And the artful elf
Promptly exclaimed about her husband's fame.
So Lotta, half-unwilling, slowly came
To conversation with him. When she went
Into the house, she found the evening spent.

Theodore arrived quite wearied out and teased,
With all excitement in him burned away.
It had gone well, he said, the audience pleased,
And he had played his very best today,
But afterwards he had been forced to stay
And practise with the stupid ones. His head
Ached furiously, and he must get to bed.

Part Second

Herr Concert-Meister Altgelt played,
And the four strings of his violin
Were spinning like bees on a day in Spring.
The notes rose into the wide sun-mote
Which slanted through the window,
They lay like coloured beads a-row,
They knocked together and parted,
And started to dance,
Skipping, tripping, each one slipping
Under and over the others so
That the polychrome fire streamed like a lance
Or a comet's tail,
Behind them.
Then a wail arose—crescendo—
And dropped from off the end of the bow,
And the dancing stopped.
A scent of lilies filled the room,
Long and slow. Each large white bloom
Breathed a sound which was holy perfume from a blessed censer,
And the hum of an organ tone,
And they waved like fans in a hall of stone

Over a bier standing there in the centre, alone.
Each lily bent slowly as it was blown.
Like smoke they rose from the violin—
Then faded as a swifter bowing
Jumbled the notes like wavelets flowing
In a splashing, pashing, rippling motion
Between broad meadows to an ocean
Wide as a day and blue as a flower,
Where every hour
Gulls dipped, and scattered, and squawked, and squealed,
And over the marshes the Angelus pealed,
And the prows of the fishing-boats were spattered
With spray.
And away a couple of frigates were starting
To race to Java with all sails set,
Topgallants, and royals, and stunsails, and jibs,
And wide moonsails; and the shining rails
Were polished so bright they sparked in the sun.
All the sails went up with a run:
    "They call me Hanging Johnny,
        Away-i-oh;
    They call me Hanging Johnny,
        So hang, boys, hang."
And the sun had set and the high moon whitened,
And the ship heeled over to the breeze.
He drew her into the shade of the sails,
And whispered tales
Of voyages in the China seas,
And his arm around her
Held and bound her.
She almost swooned,
With the breeze and the moon
And the slipping sea,
And he beside her,
Touching her, leaning—
The ship careening,
With the white moon steadily shining over
Her and her lover,
Theodore, still her lover!

Then a quiver fell on the crowded notes,
And slowly floated
A single note which spread and spread
Till it filled the room with a shimmer like gold,
And noises shivered throughout its length,
And tried its strength.
They pulled it, and tore it,
And the stuff waned thinner, but still it bore it.
Then a wide rent
Split the arching tent,
And balls of fire spurted through,
Spitting yellow, and mauve, and blue.
One by one they were quenched as they fell,
Only the blue burned steadily.
Paler and paler it grew, and—faded—away.
  Herr Altgelt stopped.

"Well, Lottachen, my Dear, what do you say?
I think I'm in good trim. Now let's have dinner.
What's this, my Love, you're very sweet today.
I wonder how it happens I'm the winner
Of so much sweetness. But I think you're thinner;
You're like a bag of feathers on my knee.
Why, Lotta child, you're almost strangling me.

I'm glad you're going out this afternoon.
The days are getting short, and I'm so tied
At the Court Theatre my poor little bride
Has not much junketing I fear, but soon
I'll ask our manager to grant a boon.
Tonight, perhaps, I'll get a pass for you,
And when I go, why Lotta can come too.

Now dinner, Love. I want some onion soup
To whip me up till that rehearsal's over.
You know it's odd how some women can stoop!
Fraeulein Gebnitz has taken on a lover,
A Jew named Goldstein. No one can discover
If it's his money. But she lives alone
Practically. Gebnitz is a stone,

Pores over books all day, and has no ear
For his wife's singing. Artists must have men;
They need appreciation. But it's queer
What messes people make of their lives, when
They should know more. If Gebnitz finds out, then
His wife will pack. Yes, shut the door at once.
I did not feel it cold, I am a dunce."

Frau Altgelt tied her bonnet on and went
Into the streets. A bright, crisp Autumn wind
Flirted her skirts and hair. A turbulent,
Audacious wind it was, now close behind,
Pushing her bonnet forward till it twined
The strings across her face, then from in front
Slantingly swinging at her with a shunt,

Until she lay against it, struggling, pushing,
Dismayed to find her clothing tightly bound
Around her, every fold and wrinkle crushing
Itself upon her, so that she was wound
In draperies as clinging as those found
Sucking about a sea nymph on the frieze
Of some old Grecian temple. In the breeze

The shops and houses had a quality
Of hard and dazzling colour; something sharp
And buoyant, like white, puffing sails at sea.
The city streets were twanging like a harp.
Charlotta caught the movement, skippingly
She blew along the pavement, hardly knowing
Toward what destination she was going.

She fetched up opposite a jeweller's shop,
Where filigreed tiaras shone like crowns,
And necklaces of emeralds seemed to drop
And then float up again with lightness. Browns
Of striped agates struck her like cold frowns
Amid the gaiety of topaz seals,
Carved though they were with heads, and arms, and wheels.

A row of pencils knobbed with quartz or sard
Delighted her. And rings of every size
Turned smartly round like hoops before her eyes,
Amethyst-flamed or ruby-girdled, jarred
To spokes and flashing triangles, and starred
Like rockets bursting on a festal day.
Charlotta could not tear herself away.

With eyes glued tightly on a golden box,
Whose rare enamel piqued her with its hue,
Changeable, iridescent, shuttlecocks
Of shades and lustres always darting through
Its level, superimposing sheet of blue,
Charlotta did not hear footsteps approaching.
She started at the words: "Am I encroaching?"

"Oh, Heinrich, how you frightened me! I thought
We were to meet at three, is it quite that?"
"No, it is not," he answered, "but I've caught
The trick of missing you. One thing is flat,
I cannot go on this way. Life is what
Might best be conjured up by the word: 'Hell'.
Dearest, when will you come?" Lotta, to quell

His effervescence, pointed to the gems
Within the window, asked him to admire
A bracelet or a buckle. But one stems
Uneasily the burning of a fire.
Heinrich was chafing, pricked by his desire.
Little by little she wooed him to her mood
Until at last he promised to be good.

But here he started on another tack;
To buy a jewel, which one would Lotta choose.
She vainly urged against him all her lack
Of other trinkets. Should she dare to use
A ring or brooch her husband might accuse
Her of extravagance, and ask to see
A strict accounting, or still worse might be.

But Heinrich would not be persuaded. Why
Should he not give her what he liked? And in
He went, determined certainly to buy
A thing so beautiful that it would win
Her wavering fancy. Altgelt's violin
He would outscore by such a handsome jewel
That Lotta could no longer be so cruel!

Pity Charlotta, torn in diverse ways.
If she went in with him, the shopman might
Recognize her, give her her name; in days
To come he could denounce her. In her fright
She almost fled. But Heinrich would be quite
Capable of pursuing. By and by
She pushed the door and entered hurriedly.

It took some pains to keep him from bestowing
A pair of ruby earrings, carved like roses,
The setting twined to represent the growing
Tendrils and leaves, upon her. "Who supposes
I could obtain such things! It simply closes
All comfort for me." So he changed his mind
And bought as slight a gift as he could find.

A locket, frosted over with seed pearls,
Oblong and slim, for wearing at the neck,
Or hidden in the bosom; their joined curls
Should lie in it. And further to bedeck
His love, Heinrich had picked a whiff, a fleck,
The merest puff of a thin, linked chain
To hang it from. Lotta could not refrain

From weeping as they sauntered down the street.
She did not want the locket, yet she did.
To have him love her she found very sweet,
But it is hard to keep love always hid.
Then there was something in her heart which chid
Her, told her she loved Theodore in him,
That all these meetings were a foolish whim.
She thought of Theodore and the life they led,

So near together, but so little mingled.
The great clouds bulged and bellied overhead,
And the fresh wind about her body tingled;
The crane of a large warehouse creaked and jingled;
Charlotta held her breath for very fear,
About her in the street she seemed to hear:
    "They call me Hanging Johnny,
        Away-i-oh;
    They call me Hanging Johnny,
        So hang, boys, hang."

And it was Theodore, under the racing skies,
Who held her and who whispered in her ear.
She knew her heart was telling her no lies,
Beating and hammering. He was so dear,
The touch of him would send her in a queer
Swoon that was half an ecstasy. And yearning
For Theodore, she wandered, slowly turning

Street after street as Heinrich wished it so.
He had some aim, she had forgotten what.
Their progress was confused and very slow,
But at the last they reached a lonely spot,
A garden far above the highest shot
Of soaring steeple. At their feet, the town
Spread open like a chequer-board laid down.

Lotta was dimly conscious of the rest,
Vaguely remembered how he clasped the chain
About her neck. She treated it in jest,
And saw his face cloud over with sharp pain.
Then suddenly she felt as though a strain
Were put upon her, collared like a slave,
Leashed in the meshes of this thing he gave.

She seized the flimsy rings with both her hands
To snap it, but they held with odd persistence.
Her eyes were blinded by two wind-blown strands
Of hair which had been loosened. Her resistance

Melted within her, from remotest distance,
Misty, unreal, his face grew warm and near,
And giving way she knew him very dear.

For long he held her, and they both gazed down
At the wide city, and its blue, bridged river.
From wooing he jested with her, snipped the blown
Strands of her hair, and tied them with a sliver
Cut from his own head. But she gave a shiver
When, opening the locket, they were placed
Under the glass, commingled and enlaced.

"When will you have it so with us?" He sighed.
She shook her head. He pressed her further. "No,
No, Heinrich, Theodore loves me," and she tried
To free herself and rise. He held her so,
Clipped by his arms, she could not move nor go.
"But you love me," he whispered, with his face
Burning against her through her kerchief's lace.

Frau Altgelt knew she toyed with fire, knew
That what her husband lit this other man
Fanned to hot flame. She told herself that few
Women were so discreet as she, who ran
No danger since she knew what things to ban.
She opened her house door at five o'clock,
A short half-hour before her husband's knock.

Part Third

The 'Residenz-Theater' sparked and hummed
With lights and people. Gebnitz was to sing,
That rare soprano. All the fiddles strummed
With tuning up; the wood-winds made a ring
Of reedy bubbling noises, and the sting
Of sharp, red brass pierced every ear-drum; patting
From muffled tympani made a dark slatting

Across the silver shimmering of flutes;
A bassoon grunted, and an oboe wailed;
The 'celli pizzicato-ed like great lutes,
And mutterings of double basses trailed
Away to silence, while loud harp-strings hailed
Their thin, bright colours down in such a scatter
They lost themselves amid the general clatter.

Frau Altgelt in the gallery, alone,
Felt lifted up into another world.
Before her eyes a thousand candles shone
In the great chandeliers. A maze of curled
And powdered periwigs past her eyes swirled.
She smelt the smoke of candles guttering,
And caught the glint of jewelled fans fluttering

All round her in the boxes. Red and gold,
The house, like rubies set in filigree,
Filliped the candlelight about, and bold
Young sparks with eye-glasses, unblushingly
Ogled fair beauties in the balcony.
An officer went by, his steel spurs jangling.
Behind Charlotta an old man was wrangling

About a play-bill he had bought and lost.
Three drunken soldiers had to be ejected.
Frau Altgelt's eyes stared at the vacant post
Of Concert-Meister, she at once detected
The stir which brought him. But she felt neglected
When with no glance about him or her way,
He lifted up his violin to play.

    The curtain went up? Perhaps. If so,
    Charlotta never saw it go.
    The famous Fraeulein Gebnitz' singing
    Only came to her like the ringing
    Of bells at a festa
    Which swing in the air

And nobody realizes they are there.
They jingle and jangle,
And clang, and bang,
And never a soul could tell whether they rang,
For the plopping of guns and rockets
And the chinking of silver to spend, in one's pockets,
And the shuffling and clapping of feet,
And the loud flapping
Of flags, with the drums,
As the military comes.
It's a famous tune to walk to,
And I wonder where they're off to.
Step-step-stepping to the beating of the drums.
But the rhythm changes as though a mist
Were curling and twisting
Over the landscape.
For a moment a rhythmless, tuneless fog
Encompasses her. Then her senses jog
To the breath of a stately minuet.
Herr Altgelt's violin is set
In tune to the slow, sweeping bows, and retreats and advances,
To curtsies brushing the waxen floor as the Court dances.
Long and peaceful like warm Summer nights
When stars shine in the quiet river. And against the lights
Blundering insects knock,
And the 'Rathaus' clock
Booms twice, through the shrill sounds
Of flutes and horns in the lamplit grounds.
Pressed against him in the mazy wavering
Of a country dance, with her short breath quavering
She leans upon the beating, throbbing
Music. Laughing, sobbing,
Feet gliding after sliding feet;
His—hers—
The ballroom blurs—
She feels the air
Lifting her hair,
And the lapping of water on the stone stair.
He is there! He is there!

Twang harps, and squeal, you thin violins,
That the dancers may dance, and never discover
The old stone stair leading down to the river
With the chestnut-tree branches hanging over
Her and her lover.
Theodore, still her lover!

The evening passed like this, in a half faint,
Delirium with waking intervals
Which were the entr'acts. Under the restraint
Of a large company, the constant calls
For oranges or syrops from the stalls
Outside, the talk, the passing to and fro,
Lotta sat ill at ease, incognito.

She heard the Gebnitz praised, the tenor lauded,
The music vaunted as most excellent.
The scenery and the costumes were applauded,
The latter it was whispered had been sent
From Italy. The Herr Direktor spent
A fortune on them, so the gossips said.
Charlotta felt a lightness in her head.

When the next act began, her eyes were swimming,
Her prodded ears were aching and confused.
The first notes from the orchestra sent skimming
Her outward consciousness. Her brain was fused
Into the music, Theodore's music! Used
To hear him play, she caught his single tone.
For all she noticed they two were alone.

Part Fourth

Frau Altgelt waited in the chilly street,
Hustled by lackeys who ran up and down
Shouting their coachmen's names; forced to retreat
A pace or two by lurching chairmen; thrown
Rudely aside by linkboys; boldly shown
The ogling rapture in two bleary eyes
Thrust close to hers in most unpleasant wise.

Escaping these, she hit a liveried arm,
Was sworn at by this glittering gentleman
And ordered off. However, no great harm
Came to her. But she looked a trifle wan
When Theodore, her belated guardian,
Emerged. She snuggled up against him, trembling,
Half out of fear, half out of the assembling

Of all the thoughts and needs his playing had given.
Had she enjoyed herself, he wished to know.
"Oh! Theodore, can't you feel that it was Heaven!"
"Heaven! My Lottachen, and was it so?
Gebnitz was in good voice, but all the flow
Of her last aria was spoiled by Klops,
A wretched flutist, she was mad as hops."

He was so simple, so matter-of-fact,
Charlotta Altgelt knew not what to say
To bring him to her dream. His lack of tact
Kept him explaining all the homeward way
How this thing had gone well, that badly. "Stay,
Theodore!" she cried at last. "You know to me
Nothing was real, it was an ecstasy."

And he was heartily glad she had enjoyed
Herself so much, and said so. "But it's good
To be got home again." He was employed
In looking at his violin, the wood
Was old, and evening air did it no good.
But when he drew up to the table for tea
Something about his wife's vivacity

Struck him as hectic, worried him in short.
He talked of this and that but watched her close.
Tea over, he endeavoured to extort
The cause of her excitement. She arose
And stood beside him, trying to compose
Herself, all whipt to quivering, curdled life,
And he, poor fool, misunderstood his wife.

Suddenly, broken through her anxious grasp,
Her music-kindled love crashed on him there.
Amazed, he felt her fling against him, clasp
Her arms about him, weighing down his chair,
Sobbing out all her hours of despair.
"Theodore, a woman needs to hear things proved.
Unless you tell me, I feel I'm not loved."

Theodore went under in this tearing wave,
He yielded to it, and its headlong flow
Filled him with all the energy she gave.
He was a youth again, and this bright glow,
This living, vivid joy he had to show
Her what she was to him. Laughing and crying,
She asked assurances there's no denying.

Over and over again her questions, till
He quite convinced her, every now and then
She kissed him, shivering as though doubting still.
But later when they were composed and when
She dared relax her probings, "Lottachen,"
He asked, "how is it your love has withstood
My inadvertence? I was made of wood."

She told him, and no doubt she meant it truly,
That he was sun, and grass, and wind, and sky
To her. And even if conscience were unruly
She salved it by neat sophistries, but why
Suppose her insincere, it was no lie
She said, for Heinrich was as much forgot
As though he'd never been within earshot.

But Theodore's hands in straying and caressing
Fumbled against the locket where it lay
Upon her neck. "What is this thing I'm pressing?"
He asked. "Let's bring it to the light of day."
He lifted up the locket. "It should stay
Outside, my Dear. Your mother has good taste.
To keep it hidden surely is a waste."

Pity again Charlotta, straight aroused
Out of her happiness. The locket brought
A chilly jet of truth upon her, soused
Under its icy spurting she was caught,
And choked, and frozen. Suddenly she sought
The clasp, but with such art was this contrived
Her fumbling fingers never once arrived

Upon it. Feeling, twisting, round and round,
She pulled the chain quite through the locket's ring
And still it held. Her neck, encompassed, bound,
Chafed at the sliding meshes. Such a thing
To hurl her out of joy! A gilded string
Binding her folly to her, and those curls
Which lay entwined beneath the clustered pearls!

Again she tried to break the cord. It stood.
"Unclasp it, Theodore," she begged. But he
Refused, and being in a happy mood,
Twitted her with her inefficiency,
Then looking at her very seriously:
"I think, Charlotta, it is well to have
Always about one what a mother gave.

As she has taken the great pains to send
This jewel to you from Dresden, it will be
Ingratitude if you do not intend
To carry it about you constantly.
With her fine taste you cannot disagree,
The locket is most beautifully designed."
He opened it and there the curls were, twined.

Charlotta's heart dropped beats like knitting-stitches.
She burned a moment, flaming; then she froze.
Her face was jerked by little, nervous twitches,
She heard her husband asking: "What are those?"
Put out her hand quickly to interpose,
But stopped, the gesture half-complete, astounded
At the calm way the question was propounded.

AMY LOWELL

"A pretty fancy, Dear, I do declare.
Indeed I will not let you put it off.
A lovely thought: yours and your mother's hair!"
Charlotta hid a gasp under a cough.
"Never with my connivance shall you doff
This charming gift." He kissed her on the cheek,
And Lotta suffered him, quite crushed and meek.

When later in their room she lay awake,
Watching the moonlight slip along the floor,
She felt the chain and wept for Theodore's sake.
She had loved Heinrich also, and the core
Of truth, unlovely, startled her. Wherefore
She vowed from now to break this double life
And see herself only as Theodore's wife.

Part Fifth

It was no easy matter to convince
Heinrich that it was finished. Hard to say
That though they could not meet (he saw her wince)
She still must keep the locket to allay
Suspicion in her husband. She would pay
Him from her savings bit by bit—the oath
He swore at that was startling to them both.

Her resolution taken, Frau Altgelt
Adhered to it, and suffered no regret.
She found her husband all that she had felt
His music to contain. Her days were set
In his as though she were an amulet
Cased in bright gold. She joyed in her confining;
Her eyes put out her looking-glass with shining.

Charlotta was so gay that old, dull tasks
Were furbished up to seem like rituals.
She baked and brewed as one who only asks
The right to serve. Her daily manuals
Of prayer were duties, and her festivals

When Theodore praised some dish, or frankly said
She had a knack in making up a bed.

So Autumn went, and all the mountains round
The city glittered white with fallen snow,
For it was Winter. Over the hard ground
Herr Altgelt's footsteps came, each one a blow.
On the swept flags behind the currant row
Charlotta stood to greet him. But his lip
Only flicked hers. His Concert-Meistership

Was first again. This evening he had got
Important news. The opera ordered from
Young Mozart was arrived. That old despot,
The Bishop of Salzburg, had let him come
Himself to lead it, and the parts, still hot
From copying, had been tried over. Never
Had any music started such a fever.

The orchestra had cheered till they were hoarse,
The singers clapped and clapped. The town was made,
With such a great attraction through the course
Of Carnival time. In what utter shade
All other cities would be left! The trade
In music would all drift here naturally.
In his excitement he forgot his tea.

Lotta was forced to take his cup and put
It in his hand. But still he rattled on,
Sipping at intervals. The new catgut
Strings he was using gave out such a tone
The "Maestro" had remarked it, and had gone
Out of his way to praise him. Lotta smiled,
He was as happy as a little child.

From that day on, Herr Altgelt, more and more,
Absorbed himself in work. Lotta at first
Was patient and well-wishing. But it wore
Upon her when two weeks had brought no burst
Of loving from him. Then she feared the worst;

AMY LOWELL

That his short interest in her was a light
Flared up an instant only in the night.

'Idomeneo' was the opera's name,
A name that poor Charlotta learnt to hate.
Herr Altgelt worked so hard he seldom came
Home for his tea, and it was very late,
Past midnight sometimes, when he knocked. His state
Was like a flabby orange whose crushed skin
Is thin with pulling, and all dented in.

He practised every morning and her heart
Followed his bow. But often she would sit,
While he was playing, quite withdrawn apart,
Absently fingering and touching it,
The locket, which now seemed to her a bit
Of some gone youth. His music drew her tears,
And through the notes he played, her dreading ears

Heard Heinrich's voice, saying he had not changed;
Beer merchants had no ecstasies to take
Their minds off love. So far her thoughts had ranged
Away from her stern vow, she chanced to take
Her way, one morning, quite by a mistake,
Along the street where Heinrich had his shop.
What harm to pass it since she should not stop!

It matters nothing how one day she met
Him on a bridge, and blushed, and hurried by.
Nor how the following week he stood to let
Her pass, the pavement narrowing suddenly.
How once he took her basket, and once he
Pulled back a rearing horse who might have struck
Her with his hoofs. It seemed the oddest luck

How many times their business took them each
Right to the other. Then at last he spoke,
But she would only nod, he got no speech
From her. Next time he treated it in joke,
And that so lightly that her vow she broke

And answered. So they drifted into seeing
Each other as before. There was no fleeing.

Christmas was over and the Carnival
Was very near, and tripping from each tongue
Was talk of the new opera. Each book-stall
Flaunted it out in bills, what airs were sung,
What singers hired. Pictures of the young
"Maestro" were for sale. The town was mad.
Only Charlotta felt depressed and sad.

Each day now brought a struggle 'twixt her will
And Heinrich's. 'Twixt her love for Theodore
And him. Sometimes she wished to kill
Herself to solve her problem. For a score
Of reasons Heinrich tempted her. He bore
Her moods with patience, and so surely urged
Himself upon her, she was slowly merged

Into his way of thinking, and to fly
With him seemed easy. But next morning would
The Stradivarius undo her mood.
Then she would realize that she must cleave
Always to Theodore. And she would try
To convince Heinrich she should never leave,
And afterwards she would go home and grieve.

All thought in Munich centered on the part
Of January when there would be given
'Idomeneo' by Wolfgang Mozart.
The twenty-ninth was fixed. And all seats, even
Those almost at the ceiling, which were driven
Behind the highest gallery, were sold.
The inches of the theatre went for gold.

Herr Altgelt was a shadow worn so thin
With work, he hardly printed black behind
The candle. He and his old violin
Made up one person. He was not unkind,

But dazed outside his playing, and the rind,
The pine and maple of his fiddle, guarded
A part of him which he had quite discarded.

    It woke in the silence of frost-bright nights,
    In little lights,
    Like will-o'-the-wisps flickering, fluttering,
    Here—there—
    Spurting, sputtering,
    Fading and lighting,
    Together, asunder—
    Till Lotta sat up in bed with wonder,
    And the faint grey patch of the window shone
    Upon her sitting there, alone.
    For Theodore slept.

The twenty-eighth was last rehearsal day,
'Twas called for noon, so early morning meant
Herr Altgelt's only time in which to play
His part alone. Drawn like a monk who's spent
Himself in prayer and fasting, Theodore went
Into the kitchen, with a weary word
Of cheer to Lotta, careless if she heard.

    Lotta heard more than his spoken word.
    She heard the vibrating of strings and wood.
    She was washing the dishes, her hands all suds,
    When the sound began,
    Long as the span
    Of a white road snaking about a hill.
    The orchards are filled
    With cherry blossoms at butterfly poise.
    Hawthorn buds are cracking,
    And in the distance a shepherd is clacking
    His shears, snip-snipping the wool from his sheep.
    The notes are asleep,
    Lying adrift on the air
    In level lines
    Like sunlight hanging in pines and pines,

Strung and threaded,
All imbedded
In the blue-green of the hazy pines.
Lines—long, straight lines!
And stems,
Long, straight stems
Pushing up
To the cup of blue, blue sky.
Stems growing misty
With the many of them,
Red-green mist
Of the trees,
And these
Wood-flavoured notes.
The back is maple and the belly is pine.
The rich notes twine
As though weaving in and out of leaves,
Broad leaves
Flapping slowly like elephants' ears,
Waving and falling.
Another sound peers
Through little pine fingers,
And lingers, peeping.
Ping! Ping! pizzicato, something is cheeping.
There is a twittering up in the branches,
A chirp and a lilt,
And crimson atilt on a swaying twig.
Wings! Wings!
And a little ruffled-out throat which sings.
The forest bends, tumultuous
With song.
The woodpecker knocks,
And the song-sparrow trills,
Every fir, and cedar, and yew
Has a nest or a bird,
It is quite absurd
To hear them cutting across each other:
Peewits, and thrushes, and larks, all at once,
And a loud cuckoo is trying to smother

A wood-pigeon perched on a birch,
"Roo—coo—oo—oo—"
"Cuckoo! Cuckoo! That's one for you!"
A blackbird whistles, how sharp, how shrill!
And the great trees toss
And leaves blow down,
You can almost hear them splash on the ground.
The whistle again:
It is double and loud!
The leaves are splashing,
And water is dashing
Over those creepers, for they are shrouds;
And men are running up them to furl the sails,
For there is a capful of wind today,
And we are already well under way.
The deck is aslant in the bubbling breeze.
"Theodore, please.
Oh, Dear, how you tease!"
And the boatswain's whistle sounds again,
And the men pull on the sheets:
    "My name is Hanging Johnny,
        Away-i-oh;
    They call me Hanging Johnny,
        So hang, boys, hang."
The trees of the forest are masts, tall masts;
They are swinging over
Her and her lover.
Almost swooning
Under the ballooning canvas,
She lies
Looking up in his eyes
As he bends farther over.
Theodore, still her lover!

The suds were dried upon Charlotta's hands,
She leant against the table for support,
Wholly forgotten. Theodore's eyes were brands
Burning upon his music. He stopped short.
Charlotta almost heard the sound of bands

Snapping. She put one hand up to her heart,
Her fingers touched the locket with a start.

Herr Altgelt put his violin away
Listlessly. "Lotta, I must have some rest.
The strain will be a hideous one today.
Don't speak to me at all. It will be best
If I am quiet till I go." And lest
She disobey, he left her. On the stairs
She heard his mounting steps. What use were prayers!

He could not hear, he was not there, for she
Was married to a mummy, a machine.
Her hand closed on the locket bitterly.
Before her, on a chair, lay the shagreen
Case of his violin. She saw the clean
Sun flash the open clasp. The locket's edge
Cut at her fingers like a pushing wedge.

A heavy cart went by, a distant bell
Chimed ten, the fire flickered in the grate.
She was alone. Her throat began to swell
With sobs. What kept her here, why should she wait?
The violin she had begun to hate
Lay in its case before her. Here she flung
The cover open. With the fiddle swung

Over her head, the hanging clock's loud ticking
Caught on her ear. 'Twas slow, and as she paused
The little door in it came open, flicking
A wooden cuckoo out: "Cuckoo!" It caused
The forest dream to come again. "Cuckoo!"
Smashed on the grate, the violin broke in two.

"Cuckoo! Cuckoo!" the clock kept striking on;
But no one listened. Frau Altgelt had gone.

AMY LOWELL

The Cross-Roads

A bullet through his heart at dawn. On the table a letter signed with a woman's name. A wind that goes howling round the house, and weeping as in shame. Cold November dawn peeping through the windows, cold dawn creeping over the floor, creeping up his cold legs, creeping over his cold body, creeping across his cold face. A glaze of thin yellow sunlight on the staring eyes. Wind howling through bent branches. A wind which never dies down. Howling, wailing. The gazing eyes glitter in the sunlight. The lids are frozen open and the eyes glitter.

The thudding of a pick on hard earth. A spade grinding and crunching. Overhead, branches writhing, winding, interlacing, unwinding, scattering; tortured twinings, tossings, creakings. Wind flinging branches apart, drawing them together, whispering and whining among them. A waning, lopsided moon cutting through black clouds. A stream of pebbles and earth and the empty spade gleams clear in the moonlight, then is rammed again into the black earth. Tramping of feet. Men and horses. Squeaking of wheels.

"Whoa! Ready, Jim?"

"All ready."

Something falls, settles, is still. Suicides have no coffin.

"Give us the stake, Jim. Now."

Pound! Pound!

"He'll never walk. Nailed to the ground."

An ash stick pierces his heart, if it buds the roots will hold him. He is a part of the earth now, clay to clay. Overhead the branches sway, and writhe, and twist in the wind. He'll never walk with a bullet in his heart, and an ash stick nailing him to the cold, black ground.

Six months he lay still. Six months. And the water welled up in his body, and soft blue spots chequered it. He lay still, for the ash stick held him in place. Six months! Then her face came out of a mist of green. Pink and white and frail like Dresden china, lilies-of-the-valley at her breast, puce-coloured silk sheening about her. Under the young green leaves, the horse at a foot-pace, the high yellow wheels of the chaise scarcely turning, her face, rippling like grain a-blowing, under her puce-coloured bonnet; and burning beside her, flaming within his correct blue coat and brass buttons, is someone. What has dimmed the sun? The horse steps on a rolling stone; a wind in the branches makes a moan. The little leaves tremble and shake, turn and quake, over and over, tearing their stems. There is a shower of young leaves, and a sudden-sprung gale wails in the trees.

The yellow-wheeled chaise is rocking—rocking, and all the branches are knocking—knocking. The sun in the sky is a flat, red plate, the branches creak and grate. She screams and cowers, for the green foliage is a lowering wave surging to smother her. But she sees nothing. The stake holds firm. The body writhes, the body squirms. The blue spots widen, the flesh tears, but the stake wears well in the deep, black ground. It holds the body in the still, black ground.

Two years! The body has been in the ground two years. It is worn away; it is clay to clay. Where the heart moulders, a greenish dust, the stake is thrust. Late August it is, and night; a night flauntingly jewelled with stars, a night of shooting stars and loud insect noises. Down the road to Tilbury, silence—and the slow flapping of large leaves. Down the road to Sutton, silence—and the darkness of heavy-foliaged trees. Down the road to Wayfleet, silence—and the whirring scrape of insects in the branches. Down the road to Edgarstown, silence—and stars like stepping-stones in a pathway overhead. It is very quiet at the cross-roads, and the sign-board points the way down the four roads, endlessly points the way where nobody wishes to go.

A horse is galloping, galloping up from Sutton. Shaking the wide, still leaves as he goes under them. Striking sparks with his iron shoes; silencing the katydids. Dr. Morgan riding to a child-birth over Tilbury way; riding to deliver a woman of her first-born son. One o'clock from Wayfleet bell tower, what a shower of shooting stars! And a breeze all of a sudden, jarring the big leaves and making them jerk up and down. Dr. Morgan's hat is blown from his head, the horse swerves, and curves away from the sign-post. An oath—spurs—a blurring of grey mist. A quick left twist, and the gelding is snorting and racing down the Tilbury road with the wind dropping away behind him.

The stake has wrenched, the stake has started, the body, flesh from flesh, has parted. But the bones hold tight, socket and ball, and clamping them down in the hard, black ground is the stake, wedged through ribs and spine. The bones may twist, and heave, and twine, but

AMY LOWELL

the stake holds them still in line. The breeze goes down, and the round stars shine, for the stake holds the fleshless bones in line.

Twenty years now! Twenty long years! The body has powdered itself away; it is clay to clay. It is brown earth mingled with brown earth. Only flaky bones remain, lain together so long they fit, although not one bone is knit to another. The stake is there too, rotted through, but upright still, and still piercing down between ribs and spine in a straight line.

Yellow stillness is on the cross-roads, yellow stillness is on the trees. The leaves hang drooping, wan. The four roads point four yellow ways, saffron and gamboge ribbons to the gaze. A little swirl of dust blows up Tilbury road, the wind which fans it has not strength to do more; it ceases, and the dust settles down. A little whirl of wind comes up Tilbury road. It brings a sound of wheels and feet. The wind reels a moment and faints to nothing under the sign-post. Wind again, wheels and feet louder. Wind again—again—again. A drop of rain, flat into the dust. Drop!—Drop! Thick heavy raindrops, and a shrieking wind bending the great trees and wrenching off their leaves.

Under the black sky, bowed and dripping with rain, up Tilbury road, comes the procession. A funeral procession, bound for the graveyard at Wayfleet. Feet and wheels—feet and wheels. And among them one who is carried.

The bones in the deep, still earth shiver and pull. There is a quiver through the rotted stake. Then stake and bones fall together in a little puffing of dust.

Like meshes of linked steel the rain shuts down behind the procession, now well along the Wayfleet road.

He wavers like smoke in the buffeting wind. His fingers blow out like smoke, his head ripples in the gale. Under the sign-post, in the pouring rain, he stands, and watches another quavering figure drifting down the Wayfleet road. Then swiftly he streams after it. It flickers among the trees. He licks out and winds about them. Over, under, blown, contorted. Spindrift after spindrift; smoke following smoke. There is a wailing through the trees, a wailing of fear, and after it laughter—laughter—laughter, skirling up to the black sky. Lightning jags over the funeral procession. A heavy clap of thunder. Then darkness and rain, and the sound of feet and wheels.

A ROXBURY GARDEN

I

Hoops

Blue and pink sashes,
Criss-cross shoes,
Minna and Stella run out into the garden
To play at hoop.

Up and down the garden-paths they race,
In the yellow sunshine,
Each with a big round hoop
White as a stripped willow-wand.

Round and round turn the hoops,
Their diamond whiteness cleaving the yellow sunshine.
The gravel crunches and squeaks beneath them,
And a large pebble springs them into the air
To go whirling for a foot or two
Before they touch the earth again
In a series of little jumps.

Spring, Hoops!
Spit out a shower of blue and white brightness.
The little criss-cross shoes twinkle behind you,
The pink and blue sashes flutter like flags,
The hoop-sticks are ready to beat you.
Turn, turn, Hoops! In the yellow sunshine.
Turn your stripped willow whiteness
Along the smooth paths.

Stella sings:
    "Round and round, rolls my hoop,
    Scarcely touching the ground,
    With a swoop,
    And a bound,
    Round and round.

With a bumpety, crunching, scattering sound,
Down the garden it flies;
In our eyes
The sun lies.
See it spin
Out and in;
Through the paths it goes whirling,
About the beds curling.
Sway now to the loop,
Faster, faster, my hoop.
Round you come,
Up you come,
Quick and straight as before.
Run, run, my hoop, run,
Away from the sun."

And the great hoop bounds along the path,
Leaping into the wind-bright air.

Minna sings:
    "Turn, hoop,
    Burn hoop,
    Twist and twine
    Hoop of mine.
    Flash along,
    Leap along,
    Right at the sun.
    Run, hoop, run.
    Faster and faster,
    Whirl, twirl.
    Wheel like fire,
    And spin like glass;
    Fire's no whiter
    Glass is no brighter.
    Dance,
    Prance,
    Over and over,
    About and about,
    With the top of you under,

And the bottom at top,
But never a stop.
Turn about, hoop, to the tap of my stick,
I follow behind you
To touch and remind you.
Burn and glitter, so white and quick,
Round and round, to the tap of a stick."

The hoop flies along between the flower-beds,
Swaying the flowers with the wind of its passing.

Beside the foxglove-border roll the hoops,
And the little pink and white bells shake and jingle
Up and down their tall spires;
They roll under the snow-ball bush,
And the ground behind them is strewn with white petals;
They swirl round a corner,
And jar a bee out of a Canterbury bell;
They cast their shadows for an instant
Over a bed of pansies,
Catch against the spurs of a columbine,
Jostle the quietness from a cluster of monk's-hood.
Pat! Pat! behind them come the little criss-cross shoes,
And the blue and pink sashes stream out in flappings of colour.

Stella sings:
    "Hoop, hoop,
    Roll along,
    Faster bowl along,
    Hoop.
    Slow, to the turning,
    Now go!—Go!
    Quick!
    Here's the stick.
    Rat-a-tap-tap it,
    Pat it, flap it.
    Fly like a bird or a yellow-backed bee,
    See how soon you can reach that tree.
    Here is a path that is perfectly straight.
    Roll along, hoop, or we shall be late."

Minna sings:
    "Trip about, slip about, whip about
    Hoop.
    Wheel like a top at its quickest spin,
    Then, dear hoop, we shall surely win.
    First to the greenhouse and then to the wall
    Circle and circle,
    And let the wind push you,
    Poke you,
    Brush you,
    And not let you fall.
    Whirring you round like a wreath of mist.
    Hoopety hoop,
    Twist,
    Twist."

Tap! Tap! go the hoop-sticks,
And the hoops bowl along under a grape arbour.
For an instant their willow whiteness is green,
Pale white-green.
Then they are out in the sunshine,
Leaving the half-formed grape clusters
A-tremble under their big leaves.

"I will beat you, Minna," cries Stella,
  Hitting her hoop smartly with her stick.
"Stella, Stella, we are winning," calls Minna,
  As her hoop curves round a bed of clove-pinks.
A humming-bird whizzes past Stella's ear,
And two or three yellow-and-black butterflies
Flutter, startled, out of a pillar rose.
Round and round race the little girls
After their great white hoops.

Suddenly Minna stops.
Her hoop wavers an instant,
But she catches it up on her stick.
"Listen, Stella!"
Both the little girls are listening;

And the scents of the garden rise up quietly about them.
"It's the chaise! It's Father!
Perhaps he's brought us a book from Boston."
Twinkle, twinkle, the little criss-cross shoes
Up the garden path.
Blue—pink—an instant, against the syringa hedge.
But the hoops, white as stripped willow-wands,
Lie in the grass,
And the grasshoppers jump back and forth
Over them.

II

Battledore and Shuttlecock

The shuttlecock soars upward
In a parabola of whiteness,
Turns,
And sinks to a perfect arc.
Plat! the battledore strikes it,
And it rises again,
Without haste,
Winged and curving,
Tracing its white flight
Against the clipped hemlock-trees.
Plat!
Up again,
Orange and sparkling with sun,
Rounding under the blue sky,
Dropping,
Fading to grey-green
In the shadow of the coned hemlocks.
"Ninety-one." "Ninety-two." "Ninety-three."
The arms of the little girls
Come up—and up—
Precisely,
Like mechanical toys.
The battledores beat at nothing,
And toss the dazzle of snow

Off their parchment drums.
"Ninety-four." Plat!
"Ninety-five." Plat!
Back and forth
Goes the shuttlecock,
Icicle-white,
Leaping at the sharp-edged clouds,
Overturning,
Falling,
Down,
And down,
Tinctured with pink
From the upthrusting shine
Of Oriental poppies.

The little girls sway to the counting rhythm;
Left foot,
Right foot.
Plat! Plat!
Yellow heat twines round the handles of the battledores,
The parchment cracks with dryness;
But the shuttlecock
Swings slowly into the ice-blue sky,
Heaving up on the warm air
Like a foam-bubble on a wave,
With feathers slanted and sustaining.
Higher,
Until the earth turns beneath it;
Poised and swinging,
With all the garden flowing beneath it,
Scarlet, and blue, and purple, and white—
Blurred colour reflections in rippled water—
Changing—streaming—
For the moment that Stella takes to lift her arm.
Then the shuttlecock relinquishes,
Bows,
Descends;
And the sharp blue spears of the air
Thrust it to earth.

Again it mounts,
Stepping up on the rising scents of flowers,
Buoyed up and under by the shining heat.
Above the foxgloves,
Above the guelder-roses,
Above the greenhouse glitter,
Till the shafts of cooler air
Meet it,
Deflect it,
Reject it,
Then down,
Down,
Past the greenhouse,
Past the guelder-rose bush,
Past the foxgloves.

"Ninety-nine," Stella's battledore springs to the impact.
Plunk! Like the snap of a taut string.
"Oh! Minna!"
The shuttlecock drops zigzagedly,
Out of orbit,
Hits the path,
And rolls over quite still.
Dead white feathers,
With a weight at the end.

III

Garden Games

The tall clock is striking twelve;
And the little girls stop in the hall to watch it,
And the big ships rocking in a half-circle
Above the dial.
Twelve o'clock!
Down the side steps
Go the little girls,
Under their big round straw hats.

Minna's has a pink ribbon,
Stella's a blue,
That is the way they know which is which.
Twelve o'clock!
An hour yet before dinner.
Mother is busy in the still-room,
And Hannah is making gingerbread.

Slowly, with lagging steps,
They follow the garden-path,
Crushing a leaf of box for its acrid smell,
Discussing what they shall do,
And doing nothing.

"Stella, see that grasshopper
Climbing up the bank!
What a jump!
Almost as long as my arm."
Run, children, run.
For the grasshopper is leaping away,
In half-circle curves,
Shuttlecock curves,
Over the grasses.
Hand in hand, the little girls call to him:
    "Grandfather, grandfather gray,
    Give me molasses, or I'll throw you away."

The grasshopper leaps into the sunlight,
Golden-green,
And is gone.

"Let's catch a bee."
Round whirl the little girls,
And up the garden.
Two heads are thrust among the Canterbury bells,
Listening,
And fingers clasp and unclasp behind backs
In a strain of silence.

White bells,
Blue bells,
Hollow and reflexed.
Deep tunnels of blue and white dimness,
Cool wine-tunnels for bees.
There is a floundering and buzzing over Minna's head.

"Bend it down, Stella. Quick! Quick!"
The wide mouth of a blossom
Is pressed together in Minna's fingers.
The stem flies up, jiggling its flower-bells,
And Minna holds the dark blue cup in her hand,
With the bee
Imprisoned in it.
Whirr! Buzz! Bump!
Bump! Whiz! Bang!
Bang!!
The blue flower tears across like paper,
And a gold-black bee darts away in the sunshine.

"If we could fly, we could catch him."
The sunshine is hot on Stella's upturned face,
As she stares after the bee.
"We'll follow him in a dove chariot.
Come on, Stella."
Run, children,
Along the red gravel paths,
For a bee is hard to catch,
Even with a chariot of doves.

Tall, still, and cowled,
Stand the monk's-hoods;
Taller than the heads of the little girls.
A blossom for Minna.
A blossom for Stella.
Off comes the cowl,
And there is a purple-painted chariot;
Off comes the forward petal,
And there are two little green doves,

AMY LOWELL

With green traces tying them to the chariot.
"Now we will get in, and fly right up to the clouds.
       Fly, Doves, up in the sky,
       With Minna and me,
       After the bee."

Up one path,
Down another,
Run the little girls,
Holding their dove chariots in front of them;
But the bee is hidden in the trumpet of a honeysuckle,
With his wings folded along his back.

The dove chariots are thrown away,
And the little girls wander slowly through the garden,
Sucking the salvia tips,
And squeezing the snapdragons
To make them gape.
"I'm so hot,
Let's pick a pansy
And see the little man in his bath,
And play we're he."
A royal bath-tub,
Hung with purple stuffs and yellow.
The great purple-yellow wings
Rise up behind the little red and green man;
The purple-yellow wings fan him,
He dabbles his feet in cool green.
Off with the green sheath,
And there are two spindly legs.
"Heigho!" sighs Minna.
"Heigho!" sighs Stella.
There is not a flutter of wind,
And the sun is directly overhead.

Along the edge of the garden
Walk the little girls.
Their hats, round and yellow like cheeses,
Are dangling by the ribbons.

The grass is a tumult of buttercups and daisies;
Buttercups and daisies streaming away
Up the hill.
The garden is purple, and pink, and orange, and scarlet;
The garden is hot with colours.
But the meadow is only yellow, and white, and green,
Cool, and long, and quiet.
The little girls pick buttercups
And hold them under each other's chins.
"You're as gold as Grandfather's snuff-box.
You're going to be very rich, Minna."
"Oh-o-o! Then I'll ask my husband to give me a pair of garnet earrings
Just like Aunt Nancy's.
I wonder if he will.
I know. We'll tell fortunes.
That's what we'll do."
Plump down in the meadow grass,
Stella and Minna,
With their round yellow hats,
Like cheeses,
Beside them.
Drop,
Drop,
Daisy petals.
    "One I love,
    Two I love,
    Three I love I say. . ."
The ground is peppered with daisy petals,
And the little girls nibble the golden centres,
And play it is cake.

A bell rings.
Dinner-time;
And after dinner there are lessons.

1777

I

The Trumpet-Vine Arbour

The throats of the little red trumpet-flowers are wide open,
And the clangour of brass beats against the hot sunlight.
They bray and blare at the burning sky.
Red! Red! Coarse notes of red,
Trumpeted at the blue sky.
In long streaks of sound, molten metal,
The vine declares itself.
Clang!—from its red and yellow trumpets.
Clang!—from its long, nasal trumpets,
Splitting the sunlight into ribbons, tattered and shot with noise.

I sit in the cool arbour, in a green-and-gold twilight.
It is very still, for I cannot hear the trumpets,
I only know that they are red and open,
And that the sun above the arbour shakes with heat.
My quill is newly mended,
And makes fine-drawn lines with its point.
Down the long, white paper it makes little lines,
Just lines—up—down—criss-cross.
My heart is strained out at the pin-point of my quill;
It is thin and writhing like the marks of the pen.
My hand marches to a squeaky tune,
It marches down the paper to a squealing of fifes.
My pen and the trumpet-flowers,
And Washington's armies away over the smoke-tree to the
    Southwest.
"Yankee Doodle," my Darling! It is you against the British,
Marching in your ragged shoes to batter down King George.
What have you got in your hat? Not a feather, I wager.
Just a hay-straw, for it is the harvest you are fighting for.
Hay in your hat, and the whites of their eyes for a target!

Like Bunker Hill, two years ago, when I watched all day from the
    house-top
Through Father's spy-glass.
The red city, and the blue, bright water,
And puffs of smoke which you made.
Twenty miles away,
Round by Cambridge, or over the Neck,
But the smoke was white—white!
Today the trumpet-flowers are red—red—
And I cannot see you fighting,
But old Mr. Dimond has fled to Canada,
And Myra sings "Yankee Doodle" at her milking.
The red throats of the trumpets bray and clang in the sunshine,
And the smoke-tree puffs dun blossoms into the blue air.

II

The City of Falling Leaves

Leaves fall,
Brown leaves,
Yellow leaves streaked with brown.
They fall,
Flutter,
Fall again.
The brown leaves,
And the streaked yellow leaves,
Loosen on their branches
And drift slowly downwards.
One,
One, two, three,
One, two, five.
All Venice is a falling of Autumn leaves—
Brown,
And yellow streaked with brown.

"That sonnet, Abate,
Beautiful,

I am quite exhausted by it.
Your phrases turn about my heart
And stifle me to swooning.
Open the window, I beg.
Lord! What a strumming of fiddles and mandolins!
'Tis really a shame to stop indoors.
Call my maid, or I will make you lace me yourself.
Fie, how hot it is, not a breath of air!
See how straight the leaves are falling.
Marianna, I will have the yellow satin caught up with silver fringe,
It peeps out delightfully from under a mantle.
Am I well painted today, 'caro Abate mio'?
You will be proud of me at the 'Ridotto', hey?
Proud of being 'Cavalier Servente' to such a lady?"
"Can you doubt it, 'Bellissima Contessa'?
A pinch more rouge on the right cheek,
And Venus herself shines less. . ."
"You bore me, Abate,
I vow I must change you!
A letter, Achmet?
Run and look out of the window, Abate.
I will read my letter in peace."
The little black slave with the yellow satin turban
Gazes at his mistress with strained eyes.
His yellow turban and black skin
Are gorgeous—barbaric.
The yellow satin dress with its silver flashings
Lies on a chair
Beside a black mantle and a black mask.
Yellow and black,
Gorgeous—barbaric.
The lady reads her letter,
And the leaves drift slowly
Past the long windows.
"How silly you look, my dear Abate,
With that great brown leaf in your wig.
Pluck it off, I beg you,
Or I shall die of laughing."

A yellow wall
Aflare in the sunlight,
Chequered with shadows,
Shadows of vine leaves,
Shadows of masks.
Masks coming, printing themselves for an instant,
Then passing on,
More masks always replacing them.
Masks with tricorns and rapiers sticking out behind
Pursuing masks with plumes and high heels,
The sunlight shining under their insteps.
One,
One, two,
One, two, three,
There is a thronging of shadows on the hot wall,
Filigreed at the top with moving leaves.
Yellow sunlight and black shadows,
Yellow and black,
Gorgeous—barbaric.
Two masks stand together,
And the shadow of a leaf falls through them,
Marking the wall where they are not.
From hat-tip to shoulder-tip,
From elbow to sword-hilt,
The leaf falls.
The shadows mingle,
Blur together,
Slide along the wall and disappear.
Gold of mosaics and candles,
And night blackness lurking in the ceiling beams.
Saint Mark's glitters with flames and reflections.
A cloak brushes aside,
And the yellow of satin
Licks out over the coloured inlays of the pavement.
Under the gold crucifixes
There is a meeting of hands
Reaching from black mantles.
Sighing embraces, bold investigations,
Hide in confessionals,

Sheltered by the shuffling of feet.
Gorgeous—barbaric
In its mail of jewels and gold,
Saint Mark's looks down at the swarm of black masks;
And outside in the palace gardens brown leaves fall,
Flutter,
Fall.
Brown,
And yellow streaked with brown.

Blue-black, the sky over Venice,
With a pricking of yellow stars.
There is no moon,
And the waves push darkly against the prow
Of the gondola,
Coming from Malamocco
And streaming toward Venice.
It is black under the gondola hood,
But the yellow of a satin dress
Glares out like the eye of a watching tiger.
Yellow compassed about with darkness,
Yellow and black,
Gorgeous—barbaric.
The boatman sings,
It is Tasso that he sings;
The lovers seek each other beneath their mantles,
And the gondola drifts over the lagoon, aslant to the coming dawn.
But at Malamocco in front,
In Venice behind,
Fall the leaves,
Brown,
And yellow streaked with brown.
They fall,
Flutter,
Fall.

BRONZE TABLETS

The Fruit Shop

Cross-ribboned shoes; a muslin gown,
High-waisted, girdled with bright blue;
A straw poke bonnet which hid the frown
She pluckered her little brows into
As she picked her dainty passage through
The dusty street. "Ah, Mademoiselle,
A dirty pathway, we need rain,
My poor fruits suffer, and the shell
Of this nut's too big for its kernel, lain
Here in the sun it has shrunk again.
The baker down at the corner says
We need a battle to shake the clouds;
But I am a man of peace, my ways
Don't look to the killing of men in crowds.
Poor fellows with guns and bayonets for shrouds!
Pray, Mademoiselle, come out of the sun.
Let me dust off that wicker chair. It's cool
In here, for the green leaves I have run
In a curtain over the door, make a pool
Of shade. You see the pears on that stool—
The shadow keeps them plump and fair."
Over the fruiterer's door, the leaves
Held back the sun, a greenish flare
Quivered and sparked the shop, the sheaves
Of sunbeams, glanced from the sign on the eaves,
Shot from the golden letters, broke
And splintered to little scattered lights.
Jeanne Tourmont entered the shop, her poke
Bonnet tilted itself to rights,
And her face looked out like the moon on nights
Of flickering clouds. "Monsieur Popain, I
Want gooseberries, an apple or two,
Or excellent plums, but not if they're high;
Haven't you some which a strong wind blew?
I've only a couple of francs for you."
Monsieur Popain shrugged and rubbed his hands.

What could he do, the times were sad.
A couple of francs and such demands!
And asking for fruits a little bad.
Wind-blown indeed! He never had
Anything else than the very best.
He pointed to baskets of blunted pears
With the thin skin tight like a bursting vest,
All yellow, and red, and brown, in smears.
Monsieur Popain's voice denoted tears.
He took up a pear with tender care,
And pressed it with his hardened thumb.
"Smell it, Mademoiselle, the perfume there
Is like lavender, and sweet thoughts come
Only from having a dish at home.
And those grapes! They melt in the mouth like wine,
Just a click of the tongue, and they burst to honey.
They're only this morning off the vine,
And I paid for them down in silver money.
The Corporal's widow is witness, her pony
Brought them in at sunrise today.
Those oranges—Gold! They're almost red.
They seem little chips just broken away
From the sun itself. Or perhaps instead
You'd like a pomegranate, they're rarely gay,
When you split them the seeds are like crimson spray.
Yes, they're high, they're high, and those Turkey figs,
They all come from the South, and Nelson's ships
Make it a little hard for our rigs.
They must be forever giving the slips
To the cursed English, and when men clips
Through powder to bring them, why dainties mounts
A bit in price. Those almonds now,
I'll strip off that husk, when one discounts
A life or two in a nigger row
With the man who grew them, it does seem how
They would come dear; and then the fight
At sea perhaps, our boats have heels
And mostly they sail along at night,
But once in a way they're caught; one feels

Ivory's not better nor finer—why peels
From an almond kernel are worth two sous.
It's hard to sell them now," he sighed.
"Purses are tight, but I shall not lose.
There's plenty of cheaper things to choose."
He picked some currants out of a wide
Earthen bowl. "They make the tongue
Almost fly out to suck them, bride
Currants they are, they were planted long
Ago for some new Marquise, among
Other great beauties, before the Chateau
Was left to rot. Now the Gardener's wife,
He that marched off to his death at Marengo,
Sells them to me; she keeps her life
From snuffing out, with her pruning knife.
She's a poor old thing, but she learnt the trade
When her man was young, and the young Marquis
Couldn't have enough garden. The flowers he made
All new! And the fruits! But 'twas said that he
Was no friend to the people, and so they laid
Some charge against him, a cavalcade
Of citizens took him away; they meant
Well, but I think there was some mistake.
He just pottered round in his garden, bent
On growing things; we were so awake
In those days for the New Republic's sake.
He's gone, and the garden is all that's left
Not in ruin, but the currants and apricots,
And peaches, furred and sweet, with a cleft
Full of morning dew, in those green-glazed pots,
Why, Mademoiselle, there is never an eft
Or worm among them, and as for theft,
How the old woman keeps them I cannot say,
But they're finer than any grown this way."
Jeanne Tourmont drew back the filigree ring
Of her striped silk purse, tipped it upside down
And shook it, two coins fell with a ding
Of striking silver, beneath her gown
One rolled, the other lay, a thing

Sparked white and sharply glistening,
In a drop of sunlight between two shades.
She jerked the purse, took its empty ends
And crumpled them toward the centre braids.
The whole collapsed to a mass of blends
Of colours and stripes. "Monsieur Popain, friends
We have always been. In the days before
The Great Revolution my aunt was kind
When you needed help. You need no more;
'Tis we now who must beg at your door,
And will you refuse?" The little man
Bustled, denied, his heart was good,
But times were hard. He went to a pan
And poured upon the counter a flood
Of pungent raspberries, tanged like wood.
He took a melon with rough green rind
And rubbed it well with his apron tip.
Then he hunted over the shop to find
Some walnuts cracking at the lip,
And added to these a barberry slip
Whose acrid, oval berries hung
Like fringe and trembled. He reached a round
Basket, with handles, from where it swung
Against the wall, laid it on the ground
And filled it, then he searched and found
The francs Jeanne Tourmont had let fall.
"You'll return the basket, Mademoiselle?"
She smiled, "The next time that I call,
Monsieur. You know that very well."
'Twas lightly said, but meant to tell.
Monsieur Popain bowed, somewhat abashed.
She took her basket and stepped out.
The sunlight was so bright it flashed
Her eyes to blindness, and the rout
Of the little street was all about.
Through glare and noise she stumbled, dazed.
The heavy basket was a care.
She heard a shout and almost grazed
The panels of a chaise and pair.

AMY LOWELL

The postboy yelled, and an amazed
Face from the carriage window gazed.
She jumped back just in time, her heart
Beating with fear. Through whirling light
The chaise departed, but her smart
Was keen and bitter. In the white
Dust of the street she saw a bright
Streak of colours, wet and gay,
Red like blood. Crushed but fair,
Her fruit stained the cobbles of the way.
Monsieur Popain joined her there.
"Tiens, Mademoiselle,
        c'est le General Bonaparte, partant pour la Guerre!"

Malmaison

I

How the slates of the roof sparkle in the sun, over there, over there, beyond the high wall! How quietly the Seine runs in loops and windings, over there, over there, sliding through the green countryside! Like ships of the line, stately with canvas, the tall clouds pass along the sky, over the glittering roof, over the trees, over the looped and curving river. A breeze quivers through the linden-trees. Roses bloom at Malmaison. Roses! Roses! But the road is dusty. Already the Citoyenne Beauharnais wearies of her walk. Her skin is chalked and powdered with dust, she smells dust, and behind the wall are roses! Roses with smooth open petals, poised above rippling leaves. . . Roses. . . They have told her so. The Citoyenne Beauharnais shrugs her shoulders and makes a little face. She must mend her pace if she would be back in time for dinner. Roses indeed! The guillotine more likely.

The tiered clouds float over Malmaison, and the slate roof sparkles in the sun.

II

Gallop! Gallop! The General brooks no delay. Make way, good people, and scatter out of his path, you, and your hens, and your dogs, and your children. The General is returned from Egypt, and is come in a 'caleche' and four to visit his new property. Throw open the gates, you, Porter of Malmaison. Pull off your cap, my man, this is your master, the husband of Madame. Faster! Faster! A jerk and a jingle and they are arrived, he and she. Madame has red eyes. Fie! It is for joy at her husband's return. Learn your place, Porter. A gentleman here for two months? Fie! Fie, then! Since when have you taken to gossiping. Madame may have a brother, I suppose. That—all green, and red, and glitter, with flesh as dark as ebony—that is a slave; a bloodthirsty, stabbing, slashing heathen, come from the hot countries to cure your tongue of idle whispering.

A fine afternoon it is, with tall bright clouds sailing over the trees.

AMY LOWELL

"Bonaparte, mon ami, the trees are golden like my star, the star I pinned to your destiny when I married you. The gypsy, you remember her prophecy! My dear friend, not here, the servants are watching; send them away, and that flashing splendour, Roustan. Superb—Imperial, but. . . My dear, your arm is trembling; I faint to feel it touching me! No, no, Bonaparte, not that—spare me that—did we not bury that last night! You hurt me, my friend, you are so hot and strong. Not long, Dear, no, thank God, not long."

The looped river runs saffron, for the sun is setting. It is getting dark. Dark. Darker. In the moonlight, the slate roof shines palely milkily white.

The roses have faded at Malmaison, nipped by the frost. What need for roses? Smooth, open petals—her arms. Fragrant, outcurved petals— her breasts. He rises like a sun above her, stooping to touch the petals, press them wider. Eagles. Bees. What are they to open roses! A little shivering breeze runs through the linden-trees, and the tiered clouds blow across the sky like ships of the line, stately with canvas.

III

THE GATES STAND WIDE AT Malmaison, stand wide all day. The gravel of the avenue glints under the continual rolling of wheels. An officer gallops up with his sabre clicking; a mameluke gallops down with his charger kicking. 'Valets de pied' run about in ones, and twos, and groups, like swirled blown leaves. Tramp! Tramp! The guard is changing, and the grenadiers off duty lounge out of sight, ranging along the roads toward Paris.

The slate roof sparkles in the sun, but it sparkles milkily, vaguely, the great glass-houses put out its shining. Glass, stone, and onyx now for the sun's mirror. Much has come to pass at Malmaison. New rocks and fountains, blocks of carven marble, fluted pillars uprearing antique temples, vases and urns in unexpected places, bridges of stone, bridges of wood, arbours and statues, and a flood of flowers everywhere, new flowers, rare flowers, parterre after parterre of flowers. Indeed, the roses bloom at Malmaison. It is youth, youth untrammeled and advancing, trundling a country ahead of it as though it were a hoop. Laughter, and spur janglings in tessellated vestibules. Tripping of clocked and embroidered stockings in little low-heeled shoes over smooth grass-plots. India muslins spangled with silver patterns slide through trees—mingle—separate—white day fireflies flashing moon-brilliance in the shade of foliage.

"The kangaroos! I vow, Captain, I must see the kangaroos."

"As you please, dear Lady, but I recommend the shady linden alley and feeding the cockatoos."

"They say that Madame Bonaparte's breed of sheep is the best in all France."

"And, oh, have you seen the enchanting little cedar she planted when the First Consul sent home the news of the victory of Marengo?"

Picking, choosing, the chattering company flits to and fro. Over the trees the great clouds go, tiered, stately, like ships of the line bright with canvas.

Prisoners'-base, and its swooping, veering, racing, giggling, bumping. The First Consul runs plump into M. de Beauharnais and falls. But he picks himself up smartly, and starts after M. Isabey. Too late, M. Le Premier Consul, Mademoiselle Hortense is out after you. Quickly, my dear Sir! Stir your short legs, she is swift and eager, and as graceful as her mother. She is there, that other, playing too, but lightly, warily, bearing herself with care, rather floating out upon the air than running, never far from goal. She is there, borne up above her guests as something indefinably fair, a rose above periwinkles. A blown rose, smooth as satin, reflexed, one loosened petal hanging back and down. A rose that undulates languorously as the breeze takes it, resting upon its leaves in a faintness of perfume.

There are rumours about the First Consul. Malmaison is full of women, and Paris is only two leagues distant. Madame Bonaparte stands on the wooden bridge at sunset, and watches a black swan pushing the pink and silver water in front of him as he swims, crinkling its smoothness into pleats of changing colour with his breast. Madame Bonaparte presses against the parapet of the bridge, and the crushed roses at her belt melt, petal by petal, into the pink water.

IV

A vile day, Porter. But keep your wits about you. The Empress will soon be here. Queer, without the Emperor! It is indeed, but best not consider that. Scratch your head and prick up your ears. Divorce is not for you to debate about. She is late? Ah, well, the roads are muddy. The rain spears are as sharp as whetted knives. They dart down and down, edged and shining. Clop-trop! Clop-trop! A carriage grows out of the mist. Hist, Porter. You can keep on your hat. It is only Her Majesty's dogs and her parrot. Clop-trop! The Ladies in Waiting, Porter. Clop-trop! It is Her Majesty. At least, I suppose it is, but the blinds are drawn.

"In all the years I have served Her Majesty she never before passed the gate without giving me a smile!"

You're a droll fellow, to expect the Empress to put out her head in the pouring rain and salute you. She has affairs of her own to think about.

Clang the gate, no need for further waiting, nobody else will be coming to Malmaison tonight.

White under her veil, drained and shaking, the woman crosses the antechamber. Empress! Empress! Foolish splendour, perished to dust. Ashes of roses, ashes of youth. Empress forsooth!

Over the glass domes of the hot-houses drenches the rain. Behind her a clock ticks—ticks again. The sound knocks upon her thought with the echoing shudder of hollow vases. She places her hands on her ears, but the minutes pass, knocking. Tears in Malmaison. And years to come each knocking by, minute after minute. Years, many years, and tears, and cold pouring rain.

"I feel as though I had died, and the only sensation I have is that I am no more."

Rain! Heavy, thudding rain!

V

THE ROSES BLOOM AT MALMAISON. And not only roses. Tulips, myrtles, geraniums, camelias, rhododendrons, dahlias, double hyacinths. All the year through, under glass, under the sky, flowers bud, expand, die, and give way to others, always others. From distant countries they have been brought, and taught to live in the cool temperateness of France. There is the 'Bonapartea' from Peru; the 'Napoleone Imperiale'; the 'Josephinia Imperatrix', a pearl-white flower, purple-shadowed, the calix pricked out with crimson points. Malmaison wears its flowers as a lady wears her gems, flauntingly, assertively. Malmaison decks herself to hide the hollow within.

The glass-houses grow and grow, and every year fling up hotter reflections to the sailing sun.

The cost runs into millions, but a woman must have something to console herself for a broken heart. One can play backgammon and patience, and then patience and backgammon, and stake gold napoleons on each game won. Sport truly! It is an unruly spirit which could ask better. With her jewels, her laces, her shawls; her two hundred and twenty dresses, her fichus, her veils; her pictures, her busts, her birds. It is absurd that she cannot be happy. The Emperor smarts under the thought of her ingratitude. What could he do more? And yet she spends, spends as never before. It is ridiculous. Can she not enjoy life at a smaller figure? Was ever monarch plagued with so extravagant an ex-wife. She owes her chocolate-merchant, her candle-merchant, her sweetmeat purveyor; her grocer, her butcher, her poulterer; her architect, and the shopkeeper who sells her rouge; her perfumer, her dressmaker, her merchant of shoes. She owes for fans, plants, engravings, and chairs. She owes masons and carpenters, vintners, lingeres. The lady's affairs are in sad confusion.

And why? Why?

Can a river flow when the spring is dry?

Night. The Empress sits alone, and the clock ticks, one after one. The clock nicks off the edges of her life. She is chipped like an old bit of china; she is frayed like a garment of last year's wearing. She is soft, crinkled, like a fading rose. And each minute flows by brushing against her, shearing off another and another petal. The Empress crushes her breasts with her hands and weeps. And the tall clouds sail over Malmaison like a procession of stately ships bound for the moon.

Scarlet, clear-blue, purple epauletted with gold. It is a parade of soldiers sweeping up the avenue. Eight horses, eight Imperial harnesses, four caparisoned postilions, a carriage with the Emperor's arms on the panels. Ho, Porter, pop out your eyes, and no wonder. Where else under the Heavens could you see such splendour!

They sit on a stone seat. The little man in the green coat of a Colonel of Chasseurs, and the lady, beautiful as a satin seed-pod, and as pale. The house has memories. The satin seed-pod holds his germs of Empire. We will stay here, under the blue sky and the turreted white clouds. She draws him; he feels her faded loveliness urge him to replenish it. Her soft transparent texture woos his nervous fingering. He speaks to her of debts, of resignation; of her children, and his; he promises that she shall see the King of Rome; he says some harsh things and some pleasant. But she is there, close to him, rose toned to amber, white shot with violet, pungent to his nostrils as embalmed rose-leaves in a twilit room.

Suddenly the Emperor calls his carriage and rolls away across the looping Seine.

VI

CRYSTAL-BLUE BRIGHTNESS OVER THE GLASS-HOUSES. Crystal-blue streaks and ripples over the lake. A macaw on a gilded perch screams; they have forgotten to take out his dinner. The windows shake. Boom! Boom! It is the rumbling of Prussian cannon beyond Pecq. Roses bloom at Malmaison. Roses! Roses! Swimming above their leaves, rotting beneath them. Fallen flowers strew the unraked walks. Fallen flowers for a fallen Emperor! The General in charge of him draws back and watches. Snatches of music—snarling, sneering music of bagpipes. They say a Scotch regiment is besieging Saint-Denis. The Emperor wipes his face, or is it his eyes. His tired eyes which see nowhere the grace they long for. Josephine! Somebody asks him a question, he does not answer, somebody else does that. There are voices, but one voice he does not hear, and yet he hears it all the time. Josephine! The Emperor puts up his hand to screen his face. The white light of a bright cloud spears sharply through the linden-trees. 'Vive l'Empereur!' There are troops passing beyond the wall, troops which sing and call. Boom! A pink rose is jarred off its stem and falls at the Emperor's feet.

"Very well. I go." Where! Does it matter? There is no sword to clatter. Nothing but soft brushing gravel and a gate which shuts with a click.

"Quick, fellow, don't spare your horses."

A whip cracks, wheels turn, why burn one's eyes following a fleck of dust.

VII

OVER THE SLATE ROOF TALL clouds, like ships of the line, pass along the sky. The glass-houses glitter splotchily, for many of their lights are broken. Roses bloom, fiery cinders quenching under damp weeds. Wreckage and misery, and a trailing of petty deeds smearing over old recollections.

The musty rooms are empty and their shutters are closed, only in the gallery there is a stuffed black swan, covered with dust. When you touch it, the feathers come off and float softly to the ground. Through a chink in the shutters, one can see the stately clouds crossing the sky toward the Roman arches of the Marly Aqueduct.

The Hammers

I

Frindsbury, Kent, 1786

Bang!
Bang!
Tap!
Tap-a-tap! Rap!
All through the lead and silver Winter days,
All through the copper of Autumn hazes.
Tap to the red rising sun,
Tap to the purple setting sun.
Four years pass before the job is done.
Two thousand oak trees grown and felled,
Two thousand oaks from the hedgerows of the Weald,
Sussex had yielded two thousand oaks
With huge boles
Round which the tape rolls
Thirty mortal feet, say the village folks.
Two hundred loads of elm and Scottish fir;
Planking from Dantzig.
My! What timber goes into a ship!
Tap! Tap!
Two years they have seasoned her ribs on the ways,
Tapping, tapping.
You can hear, though there's nothing where you gaze.
Through the fog down the reaches of the river,
The tapping goes on like heart-beats in a fever.
The church-bells chime
Hours and hours,
Dropping days in showers.
Bang! Rap! Tap!
Go the hammers all the time.
They have planked up her timbers
And the nails are driven to the head;
They have decked her over,

And again, and again.
The shoring-up beams shudder at the strain.
Black and blue breeches,
Pigtails bound and shining:
Like ants crawling about,
The hull swarms with carpenters, running in and out.
Joiners, calkers,
And they are all terrible talkers.
Jem Wilson has been to sea and he tells some wonderful tales
Of whales, and spice islands,
And pirates off the Barbary coast.
He boasts magnificently, with his mouth full of nails.
Stephen Pibold has a tenor voice,
He shifts his quid of tobacco and sings:

> "The second in command was blear-eyed Ned:
>> While the surgeon his limb was a-lopping,
> A nine-pounder came and smack went his head,
>> Pull away, pull away, pull away! I say;
>> Rare news for my Meg of Wapping!"

Every Sunday
People come in crowds
(After church-time, of course)
In curricles, and gigs, and wagons,
And some have brought cold chicken and flagons
Of wine,
And beer in stoppered jugs.
"Dear! Dear! But I tell 'ee 'twill be a fine ship.
There's none finer in any of the slips at Chatham."

The third Summer's roses have started in to blow,
When the fine stern carving is begun.
Flutings, and twinings, and long slow swirls,
Bits of deal shaved away to thin spiral curls.
Tap! Tap! A cornucopia is nailed into place.
Rap-a-tap! They are putting up a railing filigreed like Irish lace.
The Three Town's people never saw such grace.
And the paint on it! The richest gold leaf!
Why, the glitter when the sun is shining passes belief.
And that row of glass windows tipped toward the sky

Are rubies and carbuncles when the day is dry.
Oh, my! Oh, my!
They have coppered up the bottom,
And the copper nails
Stand about and sparkle in big wooden pails.
Bang! Clash! Bang!
      "And he swigg'd, and Nick swigg'd,
         And Ben swigg'd, and Dick swigg'd,
      And I swigg'd, and all of us swigg'd it,
         And swore there was nothing like grog."
It seems they sing,
Even though coppering is not an easy thing.
What a splendid specimen of humanity is a true British workman,
Say the people of the Three Towns,
As they walk about the dockyard
To the sound of the evening church-bells.
And so artistic, too, each one tells his neighbour.
What immense taste and labour!
Miss Jessie Prime, in a pink silk bonnet,
Titters with delight as her eyes fall upon it,
When she steps lightly down from Lawyer Green's whisky;
Such amazing beauty makes one feel frisky,
She explains.
Mr. Nichols says he is delighted
(He is the firm);
His work is all requited
If Miss Jessie can approve.
Miss Jessie answers that the ship is "a love."
The sides are yellow as marigold,
The port-lids are red when the ports are up:
Blood-red squares like an even chequer
Of yellow asters and portulaca.
There is a wide "black strake" at the waterline
And above is a blue like the sky when the weather is fine.
The inner bulwarks are painted red.
"Why?" asks Miss Jessie. "'Tis a horrid note."
Mr. Nichols clears his throat,
And tells her the launching day is set.
He says, "Be careful, the paint is wet."

But Miss Jessie has touched it, her sprigged muslin gown
Has a blood-red streak from the shoulder down.
"It looks like blood," says Miss Jessie with a frown.

Tap! Tap! Rap!
An October day, with waves running in blue-white lines and a capful
    of wind.
Three broad flags ripple out behind
Where the masts will be:
Royal Standard at the main,
Admiralty flag at the fore,
Union Jack at the mizzen.
The hammers tap harder, faster,
They must finish by noon.
The last nail is driven.
But the wind has increased to half a gale,
And the ship shakes and quivers upon the ways.
The Commissioner of Chatham Dockyard is coming
In his ten-oared barge from the King's Stairs;
The Marine's band will play "God Save Great George Our King";
And there is to be a dinner afterwards at the Crown, with
    speeches.
The wind screeches, and flaps the flags till they pound like
    hammers.
The wind hums over the ship,
And slips round the dog-shores,
Jostling them almost to falling.
There is no time now to wait for Commissioners and marine
    bands.
Mr. Nichols has a bottle of port in his hands.
He leans over, holding his hat, and shouts to the men below:
"Let her go!"
Bang! Bang! Pound!
The dog-shores fall to the ground,
And the ship slides down the greased planking.
A splintering of glass,
And port wine running all over the white and copper stem timbers.
"Success to his Majesty's ship, the Bellerophon!"
And the red wine washes away in the waters of the Medway.

            AMY LOWELL

II

Paris, March, 1814

Fine yellow sunlight down the rue du Mont Thabor.
Ten o'clock striking from all the clock-towers of Paris.
Over the door of a shop, in gilt letters:
"Martin—Parfumeur," and something more.
A large gilded wooden something.
Listen! What a ringing of hammers!
Tap!
Tap!
Squeak!
Tap! Squeak! Tap-a-tap!
"Blaise."
"Oui, M'sieu."
"Don't touch the letters. My name stays."
"Bien, M'sieu."
"Just take down the eagle, and the shield with the bees."
"As M'sieu pleases."
Tap! Squeak! Tap!
The man on the ladder hammers steadily for a minute or two,
Then stops.
"He! Patron!
They are fastened well, Nom d'un Chien!
What if I break them?"
"Break away,
You and Paul must have them down today."
"Bien."
And the hammers start again,
Drum-beating at the something of gilded wood.
Sunshine in a golden flood
Lighting up the yellow fronts of houses,
Glittering each window to a flash.
Squeak! Squeak! Tap!
The hammers beat and rap.
A Prussian hussar on a grey horse goes by at a dash.
From other shops, the noise of striking blows:
Pounds, thumps, and whacks;

Wooden sounds: splinters—cracks.

Paris is full of the galloping of horses and the knocking of hammers.

"Hullo! Friend Martin, is business slack

That you are in the street this morning? Don't turn your back

And scuttle into your shop like a rabbit to its hole.

I've just been taking a stroll.

The stinking Cossacks are bivouacked all up and down the Champs
 Elysees.

I can't get the smell of them out of my nostrils.

Dirty fellows, who don't believe in frills

Like washing. Ah, mon vieux, you'd have to go

Out of business if you lived in Russia. So!

We've given up being perfumers to the Emperor, have we?

Blaise,

Be careful of the hen,

Maybe I can find a use for her one of these days.

That eagle's rather well cut, Martin.

But I'm sick of smelling Cossack,

Take me inside and let me put my head into a stack

Of orris-root and musk."

Within the shop, the light is dimmed to a pearl-and-green dusk

Out of which dreamily sparkle counters and shelves of glass,

Containing phials, and bowls, and jars, and dishes; a mass

Of aqueous transparence made solid by threads of gold.

Gold and glass,

And scents which whiff across the green twilight and pass.

The perfumer sits down and shakes his head:

"Always the same, Monsieur Antoine,

You artists are wonderful folk indeed."

But Antoine Vernet does not heed.

He is reading the names on the bottles and bowls,

Done in fine gilt letters with wonderful scrolls.

"What have we here? 'Eau Imperial Odontalgique.'

I must say, mon cher, your names are chic.

But it won't do, positively it will not do.

Elba doesn't count. Ah, here is another:

'Baume du Commandeur'. That's better. He needs something to
 smother

Regrets. A little lubricant, too,

Might be useful. I have it,
'Sage Oil', perhaps he'll be good now; with it we'll submit
This fine German rouge. I fear he is pale."
"Monsieur Antoine, don't rail
At misfortune. He treated me well and fairly."
"And you prefer him to Bourbons, admit it squarely."
"Heaven forbid!" Bang! Whack!
Squeak! Squeak! Crack!
CRASH!
"Oh, Lord, Martin! That shield is hash.
The whole street is covered with golden bees.
They look like so many yellow peas,
Lying there in the mud. I'd like to paint it.
'Plum pudding of Empire'. That's rather quaint, it
Might take with the Kings. Shall I try?" "Oh, Sir,
You distress me, you do." "Poor old Martin's purr!
But he hasn't a scratch in him, I know.
Now let us get back to the powders and patches.
Foolish man,
The Kings are here now. We must hit on a plan
To change all these titles as fast as we can.
'Bouquet Imperatrice'. Tut! Tut! Give me some ink—
'Bouquet de la Reine', what do you think?
Not the same receipt?
Now, Martin, put away your conceit.
Who will ever know?
'Extract of Nobility'—excellent, since most of them are killed."
"But, Monsieur Antoine—"
"You are self-willed,
Martin. You need a salve
For your conscience, do you?
Very well, we'll halve
The compliments, also the pastes and dentifrices;
Send some to the Kings, and some to the Empresses.
'Oil of Bitter Almonds'—the Empress Josephine can have that.
'Oil of Parma Violets' fits the other one pat."
Rap! Rap! Bang!
"What a hideous clatter!
Blaise seems determined to batter

That poor old turkey into bits,
And pound to jelly my excellent wits.
Come, come, Martin, you mustn't shirk.
'The night cometh soon'—etc. Don't jerk
Me up like that. 'Essence de la Valliere'—
That has a charmingly Bourbon air.
And, oh! Magnificent! Listen to this!—
'Vinaigre des Quatre Voleurs'. Nothing amiss
With that—England, Austria, Russia and Prussia!
Martin, you're a wonder,
Upheavals of continents can't keep you under."
"Monsieur Antoine, I am grieved indeed
At such levity. What France has gone through—"
"Very true, Martin, very true,
But never forget that a man must feed."
Pound! Pound! Thump!
Pound!
"Look here, in another minute Blaise will drop that bird on the
       ground."
Martin shrugs his shoulders. "Ah, well, what then?—"
Antoine, with a laugh: "I'll give you two sous for that antiquated hen."
The Imperial Eagle sells for two sous,
And the lilies go up.
          A man must choose!

III

Paris, April, 1814

Cold, impassive, the marble arch of the Place du Carrousel.
Haughty, contemptuous, the marble arch of the Place du Carrousel.
Like a woman raped by force, rising above her fate,
Borne up by the cold rigidity of hate,
Stands the marble arch of the Place du Carrousel.
Tap! Clink-a-tink!
Tap! Rap! Chink!
What falls to the ground like a streak of flame?
Hush! It is only a bit of bronze flashing in the sun.
What are all those soldiers? Those are not the uniforms of France.

Alas! No! The uniforms of France, Great Imperial France, are done.
They will rot away in chests and hang to dusty tatters in barn lofts.
These are other armies. And their name?
Hush, be still for shame;
Be still and imperturbable like the marble arch.
Another bright spark falls through the blue air.
Over the Place du Carrousel a wailing of despair.
Crowd your horses back upon the people, Uhlans and Hungarian
    Lancers,
They see too much.
Unfortunately, Gentlemen of the Invading Armies, what they do not
    see, they hear.
Tap! Clink-a-tink!
Tap!
Another sharp spear
Of brightness,
And a ringing of quick metal lightness
On hard stones.
Workmen are chipping off the names of Napoleon's victories
From the triumphal arch of the Place du Carrousel.

Do they need so much force to quell the crowd?
An old Grenadier of the line groans aloud,
And each hammer tap points the sob of a woman.
Russia, Prussia, Austria, and the faded-white-lily Bourbon king
Think it well
To guard against tumult,
A mob is an undependable thing.
Ding! Ding!
Vienna is scattered all over the Place du Carrousel
In glittering, bent, and twisted letters.
Your betters have clattered over Vienna before,
Officer of his Imperial Majesty our Father-in-Law!
Tink! Tink!
A workman's chisel can strew you to the winds,
Munich.
Do they think
To pleasure Paris, used to the fall of cities,
By giving her a fall of letters!

It is a month too late.
One month, and our lily-white Bourbon king
Has done a colossal thing;
He has curdled love,
And soured the desires of a people.
Still the letters fall,
The workmen creep up and down their ladders like lizards on a wall.
Tap! Tap! Tink!
Clink! Clink!
"Oh, merciful God, they will not touch Austerlitz!
Strike me blind, my God, my eyes can never look on that.
I would give the other leg to save it, it took one.
Curse them! Curse them! Aim at his hat.
Give me the stone. Why didn't you give it to me?
I would not have missed. Curse him!
Curse all of them! They have got the 'A'!"
Ding! Ding!
"I saw the Terror, but I never saw so horrible a thing as this.
'Vive l'Empereur! Vive l'Empereur!'"
"Don't strike him, Fritz.
The mob will rise if you do.
Just run him out to the 'quai',
That will get him out of the way.
They are almost through."
Clink! Tink! Ding!
Clear as the sudden ring
Of a bell
"Z" strikes the pavement.
Farewell, Austerlitz, Tilsit, Presbourg;
Farewell, greatness departed.
Farewell, Imperial honours, knocked broadcast by the beating
    hammers of ignorant workmen.
Straight, in the Spring moonlight,
Rises the deflowered arch.
In the silence, shining bright,
She stands naked and unsubdued.
Her marble coldness will endure the march
Of decades.
Rend her bronzes, hammers;

Cast down her inscriptions.
She is unconquerable, austere,
Cold as the moon that swims above her
When the nights are clear.

IV

Croissy, Ile-de-France, June, 1815

"Whoa! Victorine.
Devil take the mare! I've never seen so vicious a beast.
She kicked Jules the last time she was here,
He's been lame ever since, poor chap."
Rap! Tap!
Tap-a-tap-a-tap! Tap! Tap!
"I'd rather be lame than dead at Waterloo, M'sieu Charles."
"Sacre Bleu! Don't mention Waterloo, and the damned grinning
    British.
We didn't run in the old days.
There wasn't any running at Jena.
Those were decent days,
And decent men, who stood up and fought.
We never got beaten, because we wouldn't be.
See!"
"You would have taught them, wouldn't you, Sergeant Boignet?
But today it's everyone for himself,
And the Emperor isn't what he was."
"How the Devil do you know that?
If he was beaten, the cause
Is the green geese in his army, led by traitors.
Oh, I say no names, Monsieur Charles,
You needn't hammer so loud.
If there are any spies lurking behind the bellows,
I beg they come out. Dirty fellows!"
The old Sergeant seizes a red-hot poker
And advances, brandishing it, into the shadows.
The rows of horses flick
Placid tails.
Victorine gives a savage kick

As the nails
Go in. Tap! Tap!
Jules draws a horseshoe from the fire
And beats it from red to peacock-blue and black,
Purpling darker at each whack.
Ding! Dang! Dong!
Ding-a-ding-dong!
It is a long time since any one spoke.
Then the blacksmith brushes his hand over his eyes,
"Well," he sighs,
"He's broke."
The Sergeant charges out from behind the bellows.
"It's the green geese, I tell you,
Their hearts are all whites and yellows,
There's no red in them. Red!
That's what we want. Fouche should be fed
To the guillotine, and all Paris dance the carmagnole.
That would breed jolly fine lick-bloods
To lead his armies to victory."
"Ancient history, Sergeant.
He's done."
"Say that again, Monsieur Charles, and I'll stun
You where you stand for a dung-eating Royalist."
The Sergeant gives the poker a savage twist;
He is as purple as the cooling horseshoes.
The air from the bellows creaks through the flues.
Tap! Tap! The blacksmith shoes Victorine,
And through the doorway a fine sheen
Of leaves flutters, with the sun between.
By a spurt of fire from the forge
You can see the Sergeant, with swollen gorge,
Puffing, and gurgling, and choking;
The bellows keep on croaking.
They wheeze,
And sneeze,
Creak! Bang! Squeeze!
And the hammer strokes fall like buzzing bees
Or pattering rain,
Or faster than these,

Like the hum of a waterfall struck by a breeze.
Clank! from the bellows-chain pulled up and down.
Clank!
And sunshine twinkles on Victorine's flank,
Starting it to blue,
Dropping it to black.
Clack! Clack!
Tap-a-tap! Tap!
Lord! What galloping! Some mishap
Is making that man ride so furiously.
"Francois, you!
Victorine won't be through
For another quarter of an hour." "As you hope to die,
Work faster, man, the order has come."
"What order? Speak out. Are you dumb?"
"A chaise, without arms on the panels, at the gate
In the far side-wall, and just to wait.
We must be there in half an hour with swift cattle.
You're a stupid fool if you don't hear that rattle.
Those are German guns. Can't you guess the rest?
Nantes, Rochefort, possibly Brest."
Tap! Tap! as though the hammers were mad.
Dang! Ding! Creak! The farrier's lad
Jerks the bellows till he cracks their bones,
And the stifled air hiccoughs and groans.
The Sergeant is lying on the floor
Stone dead, and his hat with the tricolore
Cockade has rolled off into the cinders. Victorine snorts and lays back
    her ears.
What glistens on the anvil? Sweat or tears?

V

St. Helena, May, 1821

Tap! Tap! Tap!
Through the white tropic night.
Tap! Tap!
Beat the hammers,

Unwearied, indefatigable.
They are hanging dull black cloth about the dead.
Lustreless black cloth
Which chokes the radiance of the moonlight
And puts out the little moving shadows of leaves.
Tap! Tap!
The knocking makes the candles quaver,
And the long black hangings waver
Tap! Tap! Tap!
Tap! Tap!
In the ears which do not heed.
Tap! Tap!
Above the eyelids which do not flicker.
Tap! Tap!
Over the hands which do not stir.
Chiselled like a cameo of white agate against the hangings,
Struck to brilliance by the falling moonlight,
A face!
Sharp as a frozen flame,
Beautiful as an altar lamp of silver,
And still. Perfectly still.
In the next room, the men chatter
As they eat their midnight lunches.
A knife hits against a platter.
But the figure on the bed
Between the stifling black hangings
Is cold and motionless,
Played over by the moonlight from the windows
And the indistinct shadows of leaves.

Tap! Tap!
Upholsterer Darling has a fine shop in Jamestown.
Tap! Tap!
Andrew Darling has ridden hard from Longwood to see to the work
    in his shop in Jamestown.
He has a corps of men in it, toiling and swearing,
Knocking, and measuring, and planing, and squaring,
Working from a chart with figures,
Comparing with their rules,

Setting this and that part together with their tools.
Tap! Tap! Tap!
Haste indeed!
So great is the need
That carpenters have been taken from the new church,
Joiners have been called from shaping pews and lecterns
To work of greater urgency.
Coffins!
Coffins is what they are making this bright Summer morning.
Coffins—and all to measurement.
There is a tin coffin,
A deal coffin,
A lead coffin,
And Captain Bennett's best mahogany dining-table
Has been sawed up for the grand outer coffin.
Tap! Tap! Tap!
Sunshine outside in the square,
But inside, only hollow coffins and the tapping upon them.
The men whistle,
And the coffins grow under their hammers
In the darkness of the shop.
Tap! Tap! Tap!

Tramp of men.
Steady tramp of men.
Slit-eyed Chinese with long pigtails
Bearing oblong things upon their shoulders
March slowly along the road to Longwood.
Their feet fall softly in the dust of the road;
Sometimes they call gutturally to each other and stop to shift
    shoulders.
Four coffins for the little dead man,
Four fine coffins,
And one of them Captain Bennett's dining-table!
And sixteen splendid Chinamen, all strong and able
And of assured neutrality.
Ah! George of England, Lord Bathurst & Co.
Your princely munificence makes one's heart glow.
Huzza! Huzza! For the Lion of England!

Tap! Tap! Tap!
Marble likeness of an Emperor,
Dead man, who burst your heart against a world too narrow,
The hammers drum you to your last throne
Which always you shall hold alone.
Tap! Tap!
The glory of your past is faded as a sunset fire,
Your day lingers only like the tones of a wind-lyre
In a twilit room.
Here is the emptiness of your dream
Scattered about you.
Coins of yesterday,
Double napoleons stamped with Consul or Emperor,
Strange as those of Herculaneum—
And you just dead!
Not one spool of thread
Will these buy in any market-place.
Lay them over him,
They are the baubles of a crown of mist
Worn in a vision and melted away at waking.
Tap! Tap!
His heart strained at kingdoms
And now it is content with a silver dish.
Strange World! Strange Wayfarer!
Strange Destiny!
Lower it gently beside him and let it lie.
Tap! Tap! Tap!

Two Travellers in the Place Vendome

Reign of Louis Philippe

A great tall column spearing at the sky
With a little man on top. Goodness! Tell me why?
He looks a silly thing enough to stand up there so high.

What a strange fellow, like a soldier in a play,
Tight-fitting coat with the tails cut away,
High-crowned hat which the brims overlay.

Two-horned hat makes an outline like a bow.
Must have a sword, I can see the light glow
Between a dark line and his leg. Vertigo

I get gazing up at him, a pygmy flashed with sun.
A weathercock or scarecrow or both things in one?
As bright as a jewelled crown hung above a throne.

Say, what is the use of him if he doesn't turn?
Just put up to glitter there, like a torch to burn,
A sort of sacrificial show in a lofty urn?

But why a little soldier in an obsolete dress?
I'd rather see a Goddess with a spear, I confess.
Something allegorical and fine. Why, yes—

I cannot take my eyes from him. I don't know why at all.
I've looked so long the whole thing swims. I feel he ought to fall.
Foreshortened there among the clouds he's pitifully small.

What do you say? There used to be an Emperor standing there,
With flowing robes and laurel crown. Really? Yet I declare
Those spiral battles round the shaft don't seem just his affair.

A togaed, laurelled man's I mean. Now this chap seems to feel
As though he owned those soldiers. Whew! How he makes one reel,
Swinging round above his circling armies in a wheel.

Sweeping round the sky in an orbit like the sun's,
Flashing sparks like cannon-balls from his own long guns.
Perhaps my sight is tired, but that figure simply stuns.

How low the houses seem, and all the people are mere flies.
That fellow pokes his hat up till it scratches on the skies.
Impudent! Audacious! But, by Jove, he blinds the eyes!

WAR PICTURES

The Allies

August 14th, 1914

Into the brazen, burnished sky, the cry hurls itself. The zigzagging cry of hoarse throats, it floats against the hard winds, and binds the head of the serpent to its tail, the long snail-slow serpent of marching men. Men weighed down with rifles and knapsacks, and parching with war. The cry jars and splits against the brazen, burnished sky.

This is the war of wars, and the cause? Has this writhing worm of men a cause?

Crackling against the polished sky is an eagle with a sword. The eagle is red and its head is flame.

In the shoulder of the worm is a teacher.

His tongue laps the war-sucked air in drought, but he yells defiance at the red-eyed eagle, and in his ears are the bells of new philosophies, and their tinkling drowns the sputter of the burning sword. He shrieks, "God damn you! When you are broken, the word will strike out new shoots."

His boots are tight, the sun is hot, and he may be shot, but he is in the shoulder of the worm.

A dust speck in the worm's belly is a poet.

He laughs at the flaring eagle and makes a long nose with his fingers. He will fight for smooth, white sheets of paper, and uncurdled ink. The sputtering sword cannot make him blink, and his thoughts are wet and rippling. They cool his heart.

He will tear the eagle out of the sky and give the earth tranquillity, and loveliness printed on white paper.

The eye of the serpent is an owner of mills.

He looks at the glaring sword which has snapped his machinery and struck away his men.

But it will all come again, when the sword is broken to a million dying stars, and there are no more wars.

Bankers, butchers, shop-keepers, painters, farmers—men, sway and sweat. They will fight for the earth, for the increase of the slow, sure roots of peace, for the release of hidden forces. They jibe at the eagle and his scorching sword.

One! Two!—One! Two!—clump the heavy boots. The cry hurtles against the sky.

Each man pulls his belt a little tighter, and shifts his gun to make it lighter. Each man thinks of a woman, and slaps out a curse at the eagle. The sword jumps in the hot sky, and the worm crawls on to the battle, stubbornly.

This is the war of wars, from eye to tail the serpent has one cause: PEACE!

The Bombardment

Slowly, without force, the rain drops into the city. It stops a moment on the carved head of Saint John, then slides on again, slipping and trickling over his stone cloak. It splashes from the lead conduit of a gargoyle, and falls from it in turmoil on the stones in the Cathedral square. Where are the people, and why does the fretted steeple sweep about in the sky? Boom! The sound swings against the rain. Boom, again! After it, only water rushing in the gutters, and the turmoil from the spout of the gargoyle. Silence. Ripples and mutters. Boom!

The room is damp, but warm. Little flashes swarm about from the firelight. The lustres of the chandelier are bright, and clusters of rubies leap in the bohemian glasses on the 'etagere'. Her hands are restless, but the white masses of her hair are quite still. Boom! Will it never cease to torture, this iteration! Boom! The vibration shatters a glass on the 'etagere'. It lies there, formless and glowing, with all its crimson gleams shot out of pattern, spilled, flowing red, blood-red. A thin bell-note pricks through the silence. A door creaks. The old lady speaks: "Victor, clear away that broken glass." "Alas! Madame, the bohemian glass!" "Yes, Victor, one hundred years ago my father brought it—" Boom! The room shakes, the servitor quakes. Another goblet shivers and breaks. Boom!

It rustles at the window-pane, the smooth, streaming rain, and he is shut within its clash and murmur. Inside is his candle, his table, his ink, his pen, and his dreams. He is thinking, and the walls are pierced with beams of sunshine, slipping through young green. A fountain tosses itself up at the blue sky, and through the spattered water in the basin he can see copper carp, lazily floating among cold leaves. A wind-harp in a cedar-tree grieves and whispers, and words blow into his brain, bubbled, iridescent, shooting up like flowers of fire, higher and higher. Boom! The flame-flowers snap on their slender stems. The fountain rears up in long broken spears of dishevelled water and flattens into the earth. Boom! And there is only the room, the table, the candle, and the sliding rain. Again, Boom!—Boom!—Boom! He stuffs his fingers into his ears. He sees corpses, and cries out in fright. Boom! It is night, and they are shelling the city! Boom! Boom!

A child wakes and is afraid, and weeps in the darkness. What has made the bed shake? "Mother, where are you? I am awake." "Hush, my Darling, I am here." "But, Mother, something so queer happened, the room shook." Boom! "Oh! What is it? What is the matter?" Boom! "Where is Father? I am so afraid." Boom! The child sobs and shrieks. The house trembles and creaks. Boom!

Retorts, globes, tubes, and phials lie shattered. All his trials oozing across the floor. The life that was his choosing, lonely, urgent, goaded by a hope, all gone. A weary man in a ruined laboratory, that is his story. Boom! Gloom and ignorance, and the jig of drunken brutes. Diseases like snakes crawling over the earth, leaving trails of slime. Wails from people burying their dead. Through the window, he can see the rocking steeple. A ball of fire falls on the lead of the roof, and the sky tears apart on a spike of flame. Up the spire, behind the lacings of stone, zigzagging in and out of the carved tracings, squirms the fire. It spouts like yellow wheat from the gargoyles, coils round the head of Saint John, and aureoles him in light. It leaps into the night and hisses against the rain. The Cathedral is a burning stain on the white, wet night.

Boom! The Cathedral is a torch, and the houses next to it begin to scorch. Boom! The bohemian glass on the 'etagere' is no longer there. Boom! A stalk of flame sways against the red damask curtains. The old lady cannot walk. She watches the creeping stalk and counts. Boom!— Boom!—Boom!

The poet rushes into the street, and the rain wraps him in a sheet of silver. But it is threaded with gold and powdered with scarlet beads. The city burns. Quivering, spearing, thrusting, lapping, streaming, run the flames. Over roofs, and walls, and shops, and stalls. Smearing its gold on the sky, the fire dances, lances itself through the doors, and lisps and chuckles along the floors.

The child wakes again and screams at the yellow petalled flower flickering at the window. The little red lips of flame creep along the ceiling beams.

The old man sits among his broken experiments and looks at the burning Cathedral. Now the streets are swarming with people. They seek shelter and crowd into the cellars. They shout and call, and over all, slowly and without force, the rain drops into the city. Boom! And the steeple crashes down among the people. Boom! Boom, again! The water rushes along the gutters. The fire roars and mutters. Boom!

LEAD SOLDIERS

The nursery fire burns brightly, crackling in cheerful little explosions and trails of sparks up the back of the chimney. Miniature rockets peppering the black bricks with golden stars, as though a gala flamed a night of victorious wars.

The nodding mandarin on the bookcase moves his head forward and back, slowly, and looks into the air with his blue-green eyes. He stares into the air and nods—forward and back. The red rose in his hand is a crimson splash on his yellow coat. Forward and back, and his blue-green eyes stare into the air, and he nods—nods.

Tommy's soldiers march to battle,
Trumpets flare and snare-drums rattle.
Bayonets flash, and sabres glance—
How the horses snort and prance!
Cannon drawn up in a line
Glitter in the dizzy shine
Of the morning sunlight. Flags
Ripple colours in great jags.
Red blows out, then blue, then green,
Then all three—a weaving sheen
Of prismed patriotism. March
Tommy's soldiers, stiff and starch,
Boldly stepping to the rattle
Of the drums, they go to battle.

Tommy lies on his stomach on the floor and directs his columns. He puts his infantry in front, and before them ambles a mounted band. Their instruments make a strand of gold before the scarlet-tunicked soldiers, and they take very long steps on their little green platforms, and from the ranks bursts the song of Tommy's soldiers marching to battle. The song jolts a little as the green platforms stick on the thick carpet. Tommy wheels his guns round the edge of a box of blocks, and places a squad of cavalry on the commanding eminence of a footstool.

The fire snaps pleasantly, and the old Chinaman nods—nods. The fire makes the red rose in his hand glow and twist. Hist! That is a bold song Tommy's soldiers sing as they march along to battle.

Crack! Rattle! The sparks fly up the chimney.

> *Tommy's army's off to war—*
> *Not a soldier knows what for.*
> *But he knows about his rifle,*
> *How to shoot it, and a trifle*
> *Of the proper thing to do*
> *When it's he who is shot through.*
> *Like a cleverly trained flea,*
> *He can follow instantly*
> *Orders, and some quick commands*
> *Really make severe demands*
> *On a mind that's none too rapid,*
> *Leaden brains tend to the vapid.*
> *But how beautifully dressed*
> *Is this army! How impressed*
> *Tommy is when at his heel*
> *All his baggage wagons wheel*
> *About the patterned carpet, and*
> *Moving up his heavy guns*
> *He sees them glow with diamond suns*
> *Flashing all along each barrel.*
> *And the gold and blue apparel*
> *Of his gunners is a joy.*
> *Tommy is a lucky boy.*
> *Boom! Boom! Ta-ra!*

The old mandarin nods under his purple umbrella. The rose in his hand shoots its petals up in thin quills of crimson. Then they collapse and shrivel like red embers. The fire sizzles.

Tommy is galloping his cavalry, two by two, over the floor. They must pass the open terror of the door and gain the enemy encamped under the wash-stand. The mounted band is very grand, playing allegro and leading the infantry on at the double quick. The tassel of the hearth-rug has flung down the bass-drum, and he and his dapple-grey horse lie overtripped, slipped out of line, with the little lead drumsticks glistening to the fire's shine.

The fire burns and crackles, and tickles the tripped bass-drum with its sparkles.

The marching army hitches its little green platforms valiantly, and steadily approaches the door. The overturned bass-drummer, lying on the hearth-rug, melting in the heat, softens and sheds tears. The song jeers at his impotence, and flaunts the glory of the martial and still upstanding, vaunting the deeds it will do. For are not Tommy's soldiers all bright and new?

Tommy's leaden soldiers we,
Glittering with efficiency.
Not a button's out of place,
Tons and tons of golden lace
Wind about our officers.
Every manly bosom stirs
At the thought of killing—killing!
Tommy's dearest wish fulfilling.
We are gaudy, savage, strong,
And our loins so ripe we long
First to kill, then procreate,
Doubling so the laws of Fate.
On their women we have sworn
To graft our sons. And overborne
They'll rear us younger soldiers, so
Shall our race endure and grow,
Waxing greater in the wombs
Borrowed of them, while damp tombs
Rot their men. O Glorious War!
Goad us with your points, Great Star!

The china mandarin on the bookcase nods slowly, forward and back—forward and back—and the red rose writhes and wriggles, thrusting its flaming petals under and over one another like tortured snakes.

The fire strokes them with its dartles, and purrs at them, and the old man nods.

AMY LOWELL

Tommy does not hear the song. He only sees the beautiful, new, gaily-coloured lead soldiers. They belong to him, and he is very proud and happy. He shouts his orders aloud, and gallops his cavalry past the door to the wash-stand. He creeps over the floor on his hands and knees to one battalion and another, but he sees only the bright colours of his soldiers and the beautiful precision of their gestures. He is a lucky boy to have such fine lead soldiers to enjoy.

Tommy catches his toe in the leg of the wash-stand, and jars the pitcher. He snatches at it with his hands, but it is too late. The pitcher falls, and as it goes, he sees the white water flow over its lip. It slips between his fingers and crashes to the floor. But it is not water which oozes to the door. The stain is glutinous and dark, a spark from the firelight heads it to red. In and out, between the fine, new soldiers, licking over the carpet, squirms the stream of blood, lapping at the little green platforms, and flapping itself against the painted uniforms.

The nodding mandarin moves his head slowly, forward and back. The rose is broken, and where it fell is black blood. The old mandarin leers under his purple umbrella, and nods—forward and back, staring into the air with blue-green eyes. Every time his head comes forward a rosebud pushes between his lips, rushes into full bloom, and drips to the ground with a splashing sound. The pool of black blood grows and grows, with each dropped rose, and spreads out to join the stream from the wash-stand. The beautiful army of lead soldiers steps boldly forward, but the little green platforms are covered in the rising stream of blood.

The nursery fire burns brightly and flings fan-bursts of stars up the chimney, as though a gala flamed a night of victorious wars.

The Painter on Silk

There was a man
Who made his living
By painting roses
Upon silk.

He sat in an upper chamber
And painted,
And the noises of the street
Meant nothing to him.

When he heard bugles, and fifes, and drums,
He thought of red, and yellow, and white roses
Bursting in the sunshine,
And smiled as he worked.

He thought only of roses,
And silk.
When he could get no more silk
He stopped painting
And only thought
Of roses.

The day the conquerors
Entered the city,
The old man
Lay dying.
He heard the bugles and drums,
And wished he could paint the roses
Bursting into sound.

A Ballad of Footmen

Now what in the name of the sun and the stars
Is the meaning of this most unholy of wars?

Do men find life so full of humour and joy
That for want of excitement they smash up the toy?

Fifteen millions of soldiers with popguns and horses
All bent upon killing, because their "of courses"

Are not quite the same. All these men by the ears,
And nine nations of women choking with tears.

It is folly to think that the will of a king
Can force men to make ducks and drakes of a thing

They value, and life is, at least one supposes,
Of some little interest, even if roses

Have not grown up between one foot and the other.
What a marvel bureaucracy is, which can smother

Such quite elementary feelings, and tag
A man with a number, and set him to wag

His legs and his arms at the word of command
Or the blow of a whistle! He's certainly damned,

Fit only for mince-meat, if a little gold lace
And an upturned moustache can set him to face

Bullets, and bayonets, and death, and diseases,
Because some one he calls his Emperor, pleases.

If each man were to lay down his weapon, and say,
With a click of his heels, "I wish you Good-day,"

Now what, may I ask, could the Emperor do?
A king and his minions are really so few.

Angry? Oh, of course, a most furious Emperor!
But the men are so many they need not mind his temper, or

The dire results which could not be inflicted.
With no one to execute sentence, convicted

Is just the weak wind from an old, broken bellows.
What lackeys men are, who might be such fine fellows!

To be killing each other, unmercifully,
At an order, as though one said, "Bring up the tea."

Or is it that tasting the blood on their jaws
They lap at it, drunk with its ferment, and laws

So patiently builded, are nothing to drinking
More blood, any blood. They don't notice its stinking.

I don't suppose tigers do, fighting cocks, sparrows,
And, as to men—what are men, when their marrows

Are running with blood they have gulped; it is plain
Such excellent sport does not recollect pain.

Toll the bells in the steeples left standing. Half-mast
The flags which meant order, for order is past.

Take the dust of the streets and sprinkle your head,
The civilization we've worked for is dead.

Squeeze into this archway, the head of the line
Has just swung round the corner to 'Die Wacht am Rhein'.

THE OVERGROWN PASTURE

Reaping

You want to know what's the matter with me, do yer?
My! ain't men blinder'n moles?
It ain't nothin' new, be sure o' that.
Why, ef you'd had eyes you'd ha' seed
Me changin' under your very nose,
Each day a little diff'rent.
But you never see nothin', you don't.
Don't touch me, Jake,
Don't you dars't to touch me,
I ain't in no humour.
That's what's come over me;
Jest a change clear through.
You lay still, an' I'll tell yer,
I've had it on my mind to tell yer
Fer some time.
It's a strain livin' a lie from mornin' till night,
An' I'm goin' to put an end to it right now.
An' don't make any mistake about one thing,
When I married yer I loved yer.
Why, your voice 'ud make
Me go hot and cold all over,
An' your kisses most stopped my heart from beatin'.
Lord! I was a silly fool.
But that's the way 'twas.
Well, I married yer
An' thought Heav'n was comin'
To set on the door-step.
Heav'n didn't do no settin',
Though the first year warn't so bad.
The baby's fever threw you off some, I guess,
An' then I took her death real hard,
An' a mopey wife kind o' disgusts a man.
I ain't blamin' yer exactly.
But that's how 'twas.
Do lay quiet,
I know I'm slow, but it's harder to say 'n I thought.

There come a time when I got to be
More wife agin than mother.
The mother part was sort of a waste
When we didn't have no other child.
But you'd got used ter lots o' things,
An' you was all took up with the farm.
Many's the time I've laid awake
Watchin' the moon go clear through the elm-tree,
Out o' sight.
I'd foller yer around like a dog,
An' set in the chair you'd be'n settin' in,
Jest to feel its arms around me,
So long's I didn't have yours.
It preyed on me, I guess,
Longin' and longin'
While you was busy all day, and snorin' all night.
Yes, I know you're wide awake now,
But now ain't then,
An' I guess you'll think diff'rent
When I'm done.
Do you mind the day you went to Hadrock?
I didn't want to stay home for reasons,
But you said someone 'd have to be here
'Cause Elmer was comin' to see t' th' telephone.
An' you never see why I was so set on goin' with yer,
Our married life hadn't be'n any great shakes,
Still marriage is marriage, an' I was raised God-fearin'.
But, Lord, you didn't notice nothin',
An' Elmer hangin' around all Winter!
'Twas a lovely mornin'.
The apple-trees was jest elegant
With their blossoms all flared out,
An' there warn't a cloud in the sky.
You went, you wouldn't pay no 'tention to what I said,
An' I heard the Ford chuggin' for most a mile,
The air was so still.
Then Elmer come.
It's no use your frettin', Jake,
I'll tell you all about it.

I know what I'm doin',
An' what's worse, I know what I done.
Elmer fixed th' telephone in about two minits,
An' he didn't seem in no hurry to go,
An' I don't know as I wanted him to go either,
I was awful mad at your not takin' me with yer,
An' I was tired o' wishin' and wishin'
An' gittin' no comfort.
I guess it ain't necessary to tell yer all the things.
He stayed to dinner,
An' he helped me do the dishes,
An' he said a home was a fine thing,
An' I said dishes warn't a home
Nor yet the room they're in.
He said a lot o' things,
An' I fended him off at first,
But he got talkin' all around me,
Clost up to the things I'd be'n thinkin',
What's the use o' me goin' on, Jake,
You know.
He got all he wanted,
An' I give it to him,
An' what's more, I'm glad!
I ain't dead, anyway,
An' somebody thinks I'm somethin'.
Keep away, Jake,
You can kill me to-morrer if you want to,
But I'm goin' to have my say.
Funny thing! Guess I ain't made to hold a man.
Elmer ain't be'n here for mor'n two months.
I don't want to pretend nothin',
Mebbe if he'd be'n lately
I shouldn't have told yer.
I'll go away in the mornin', o' course.
What you want the light fer?
I don't look no diff'rent.
Ain't the moon bright enough
To look at a woman that's deceived yer by?
Don't, Jake, don't, you can't love me now!

It ain't a question of forgiveness.
Why! I'd be thinkin' o' Elmer ev'ry minute;
It ain't decent.
Oh, my God! It ain't decent any more either way!

OFF THE TURNPIKE

Good ev'nin', Mis' Priest.
I jest stepped in to tell you Good-bye.
Yes, it's all over.
All my things is packed
An' every last one o' them boxes
Is on Bradley's team
Bein' hauled over to th' depot.
No, I ain't goin' back agin.
I'm stoppin' over to French's fer tonight,
And goin' down first train in th' mornin'.
Yes, it do seem kinder queer
Not to be goin' to see Cherry's Orchard no more,
But Land Sakes! When a change's comin',
Why, I al'ays say it can't come too quick.
Now, that's real kind o' you,
Your doughnuts is always so tasty.
Yes, I'm goin' to Chicago,
To my niece,
She's married to a fine man, hardware business,
An' doin' real well, she tells me.
Lizzie's be'n at me to go out ther for the longest while.
She ain't got no kith nor kin to Chicago, you know
She's rented me a real nice little flat,
Same house as hers,
An' I'm goin' to try that city livin' folks say's so pleasant.
Oh, yes, he was real generous,
Paid me a sight o' money fer the Orchard;
I told him 'twouldn't yield nothin' but stones,
But he ain't farmin' it.
Lor', no, Mis' Priest,
He's jest took it to set and look at the view.
Mebbe he wouldn't be so stuck on the view
Ef he'd seed it every mornin' and night for forty year
Same's as I have.
I dessay it's pretty enough,
But it's so pressed into me

I c'n see't with my eyes shut.
No. I ain't cold, Mis' Priest,
Don't shut th' door.
I'll be all right in a minit.
But I ain't a mite sorry to leave that view.
Well, mebbe 'tis queer to feel so,
An' mebbe 'taint.
My! But that tea's revivin'.
Old things ain't always pleasant things, Mis' Priest.
No, no, I don't cal'late on comin' back,
That's why I'd ruther be to Chicago,
Boston's too near.
It ain't cold, Mis' Priest,
It's jest my thoughts.
I ain't sick, only—
Mis' Priest, ef you've nothin' ter take yer time,
An' have a mind to listen,
Ther's somethin' I'd like ter speak about
I ain't never mentioned it,
But I'd like to tell yer 'fore I go.
Would you mind lowerin' them shades,
Fall twilight's awful grey,
An' that fire's real cosy with the shades drawed.
Well, I guess folks about here think I've be'n dret'ful onsociable.
You needn't say 'taint so, 'cause I know diff'rent.
An' what's more, it's true.
Well, the reason is I've be'n scared out o' my life.
Scared ev'ry minit o' th' time, fer eight year.
Eight mortal year 'tis, come next June.
'Twas on the eighteenth o' June,
Six months after I'd buried my husband,
That somethin' happened ter me.
Mebbe you'll mind that afore that
I was a cheery body.
Hiram was too,
Al'ays liked to ask a neighbor in,
An' ev'n when he died,
Barrin' low sperrits, I warn't averse to seein' nobody.
But that eighteenth o' June changed ev'rythin'.

I was doin' most o' th' farmwork myself,
With jest a hired boy, Clarence King, 'twas,
Comin' in fer an hour or two.
Well, that eighteenth o' June
I was goin' round,
Lockin' up and seein' to things 'fore I went to bed.
I was jest steppin' out t' th' barn,
Goin' round outside 'stead o' through the shed,
'Cause there was such a sight o' moonlight
Somehow or another I thought 'twould be pretty outdoors.
I got settled for pretty things that night, I guess.
I ain't stuck on 'em no more.
Well, them laylock bushes side o' th' house
Was real lovely.
Glitt'rin' and shakin' in the moonlight,
An' the smell o' them rose right up
An' most took my breath away.
The colour o' the spikes was all faded out,
They never keep their colour when the moon's on 'em,
But the smell fair 'toxicated me.
I was al'ays partial to a sweet scent,
An' I went close up t' th' bushes
So's to put my face right into a flower.
Mis' Priest, jest's I got breathin' in that laylock bloom
I saw, layin' right at my feet,
A man's hand!
It was as white's the side o' th' house,
And sparklin' like that lum'nous paint they put on gate-posts.
I screamed right out,
I couldn't help it,
An' I could hear my scream
Goin' over an' over
In that echo be'ind th' barn.
Hearin' it agin an' agin like that
Scared me so, I dar'sn't scream any more.
I jest stood ther,
And looked at that hand.
I thought the echo'd begin to hammer like my heart,
But it didn't.

There was only th' wind,
Sighin' through the laylock leaves,
An' slappin' 'em up agin the house.
Well, I guess I looked at that hand
Most ten minits,
An' it never moved,
Jest lay there white as white.
After a while I got to thinkin' that o' course
'Twas some drunken tramp over from Redfield.
That calmed me some,
An' I commenced to think I'd better git him out
From under them laylocks.
I planned to drag him in t' th' barn
An' lock him in ther till Clarence come in th' mornin'.
I got so mad thinkin' o' that all-fired brazen tramp
Asleep in my laylocks,
I jest stooped down and grabbed th' hand and give it an awful pull.
Then I bumped right down settin' on the ground.
Mis' Priest, ther warn't no body come with the hand.
No, it ain't cold, it's jest that I can't abear thinkin' of it,
Ev'n now.
I'll take a sip o' tea.
Thank you, Mis' Priest, that's better.
I'd ruther finish now I've begun.
Thank you, jest the same.
I dropped the hand's ef it'd be'n red hot
'Stead o' ice cold.
Fer a minit or two I jest laid on that grass
Pantin'.
Then I up and run to them laylocks
An' pulled 'em every which way.
True es I'm settin' here, Mis' Priest,
Ther warn't nothin' ther.
I peeked an' pryed all about 'em,
But ther warn't no man ther
Neither livin' nor dead.
But the hand was ther all right,
Upside down, the way I'd dropped it,
And glist'nin' fit to dazzle yer.

I don't know how I done it,
An' I don't know why I done it,
But I wanted to git that dret'ful hand out o' sight
I got in t' th' barn, somehow,
An' felt roun' till I got a spade.
I couldn't stop fer a lantern,
Besides, the moonlight was bright enough in all conscience.
Then I scooped that awful thing up in th' spade.
I had a sight o' trouble doin' it.
It slid off, and tipped over, and I couldn't bear
Ev'n to touch it with my foot to prop it,
But I done it somehow.
Then I carried it off be'ind the barn,
Clost to an old apple-tree
Where you couldn't see from the house,
An' I buried it,
Good an' deep.

I don't rec'lect nothin' more o' that night.
Clarence woke me up in th' mornin',
Hollerin' fer me to come down and set th' milk.
When he'd gone,
I stole roun' to the apple-tree
And seed the earth all new turned
Where I left it in my hurry.
I did a heap o' gardenin'
That mornin'.
I couldn't cut no big sods
Fear Clarence would notice and ask me what I wanted 'em fer,
So I got teeny bits o' turf here and ther,
And no one couldn't tell ther'd be'n any diggin'
When I got through.
They was awful days after that, Mis' Priest,
I used ter go every mornin' and poke about them bushes,
An' up and down the fence,
Ter find the body that hand come off of.
But I couldn't never find nothin'.
I'd lay awake nights
Hearin' them laylocks blowin' and whiskin'.

At last I had Clarence cut 'em down
An' make a big bonfire of 'em.
I told him the smell made me sick,
An' that warn't no lie,
I can't abear the smell on 'em now;
An' no wonder, es you say.
I fretted somethin' awful 'bout that hand
I wondered, could it be Hiram's,
But folks don't rob graveyards hereabouts.
Besides, Hiram's hands warn't that awful, starin' white.
I give up seein' people,
I was afeared I'd say somethin'.
You know what folks thought o' me
Better'n I do, I dessay,
But mebbe now you'll see I couldn't do nothin' diff'rent.
But I stuck it out,
I warn't goin' to be downed
By no loose hand, no matter how it come ther
But that ain't the worst, Mis' Priest,
Not by a long ways.
Two year ago, Mr. Densmore made me an offer for Cherry's Orchard.
Well, I'd got used to th' thought o' bein' sort o' blighted,
An' I warn't scared no more.
Lived down my fear, I guess.
I'd kinder got used to th' thought o' that awful night,
And I didn't mope much about it.
Only I never went out o' doors by moonlight;
That stuck.
Well, when Mr. Densmore's offer come,
I started thinkin' 'bout the place
An' all the things that had gone on ther.
Thinks I, I guess I'll go and see where I put the hand.
I was foolhardy with the long time that had gone by.
I know'd the place real well,
Fer I'd put it right in between two o' the apple roots.
I don't know what possessed me, Mis' Priest,
But I kinder wanted to know
That the hand had been flesh and bone, anyway.
It had sorter bothered me, thinkin' I might ha' imagined it.

AMY LOWELL

I took a mornin' when the sun was real pleasant and warm;
I guessed I wouldn't jump for a few old bones.
But I did jump, somethin' wicked.
Ther warn't no bones!
Ther warn't nothin'!
Not ev'n the gold ring I'd minded bein' on the little finger.
I don't know ef ther ever was anythin'.
I've worried myself sick over it.
I be'n diggin' and diggin' day in and day out
Till Clarence ketched me at it.
Oh, I know'd real well what you all thought,
An' I ain't sayin' you're not right,
But I ain't goin' to end in no county 'sylum
If I c'n help it.
The shiv'rin' fits come on me sudden like.
I know 'em, don't you trouble.
I've fretted considerable about the 'sylum,
I guess I be'n frettin' all the time I ain't be'n diggin'.
But anyhow I can't dig to Chicago, can I?
Thank you, Mis' Priest,
I'm better now. I only dropped in in passin'.
I'll jest be steppin' along down to French's.
No, I won't be seein' nobody in the mornin',
It's a pretty early start.
Don't you stand ther, Mis' Priest,
The wind'll blow yer lamp out,
An' I c'n see easy, I got aholt o' the gate now.
I ain't a mite tired, thank you.
Good-night.

The Grocery

"Hullo, Alice!"
"Hullo, Leon!"
"Say, Alice, gi' me a couple
 O' them two for five cigars,
 Will yer?"
"Where's your nickel?"
"My! Ain't you close!
 Can't trust a feller, can yer."
"Trust you! Why
 What you owe this store
 Would set you up in business.
 I can't think why Father 'lows it."
"Yer Father's a sight more neighbourly
 Than you be. That's a fact.
 Besides, he knows I got a vote."
"A vote! Oh, yes, you got a vote!
 A lot o' good the Senate'll be to Father
 When all his bank account
 Has run away in credits.
 There's your cigars,
 If you can relish smokin'
 With all you owe us standin'."
"I dunno as that makes 'em taste any diff'rent.
 You ain't fair to me, Alice, 'deed you ain't.
 I work when anythin's doin'.
 I'll get a carpenterin' job next Summer sure.
 Cleve was tellin' me today he'd take me on come Spring."
"Come Spring, and this December!
 I've no patience with you, Leon,
 Shilly-shallyin' the way you do.
 Here, lift over them crates o' oranges
 I wanter fix 'em in the winder."
"It riles yer, don't it, me not havin' work.
 You pepper up about it somethin' good.
 You pick an' pick, and that don't help a mite.
 Say, Alice, do come in out o' that winder.

Th' oranges c'n wait,
An' I don't like talkin' to yer back."
"Don't you! Well, you'd better make the best o' what you can git.
Maybe you won't have my back to talk to soon.
They look good in pyramids with the 'lectric light on 'em,
Don't they?
Now hand me them bananas
An' I'll string 'em right acrost."
"What do yer mean
'Bout me not havin' you to talk to?
Are yer springin' somethin' on me?"
"I don't know 'bout springin'
When I'm tellin' you right out.
I'm goin' away, that's all."
"Where? Why?
What yer mean—goin' away?"
"I've took a place
Down to Boston, in a candy store
For the holidays."
"Good Land, Alice,
What in the Heavens fer!"
"To earn some money,
And to git away from here, I guess."
"Ain't yer Father got enough?
Don't he give yer proper pocket-money?"
"He'd have a plenty, if you folks paid him."
"He's rich I tell yer.
I never figured he'd be close with you."
"Oh, he ain't. Not close.
That ain't why.
But I must git away from here.
I must! I must!"
"You got a lot o' reason in yer
Tonight.
How long d' you cal'late
You'll be gone?"
"Maybe for always."
"What ails yer, Alice?
Talkin' wild like that.

Ain't you an' me goin' to be married
 Some day."
"Some day! Some day!
 I guess the sun'll never rise on some day."
"So that's the trouble.
 Same old story.
 'Cause I ain't got the cash to settle right now.
 You know I love yer,
 An' I'll marry yer as soon
 As I c'n raise the money."
"You've said that any time these five year,
 But you don't do nothin'."
"Wot could I do?
 Ther ain't no work here Winters.
 Not fer a carpenter, ther ain't."
"I guess you warn't born a carpenter.
 Ther's ice-cuttin' a plenty."
"I got a dret'ful tender throat;
 Dr. Smiles he told me
 I mustn't resk ice-cuttin'."
"Why haven't you gone to Boston,
 And hunted up a job?"
"Have yer forgot the time I went expressin'
 In the American office, down ther?"
"And come back two weeks later!
 No, I ain't."
"You didn't want I should git hurted,
 Did yer?
 I'm a sight too light fer all that liftin' work.
 My back was commencin' to strain, as 'twas.
 Ef I was like yer brother now,
 I'd ha' be'n down to the city long ago.
 But I'm too clumsy fer a dancer.
 I ain't got Arthur's luck."
"Do you call it luck to be a disgrace to your folks,
 And git locked up in jail!"
"Oh, come now, Alice,
 'Disgrace' is a mite strong.
 Why, the jail was a joke.

Art's all right."
"All right!
All right to dance, and smirk, and lie
For a livin',
And then in the end
Lead a silly girl to give you
What warn't hers to give
By pretendin' you'd marry her—
And she a pupil."
"He'd ha' married her right enough,
Her folks was millionaires."
"Yes, he'd ha' married her!
Thank God, they saved her that."
"Art's a fine feller.
I wish I had his luck.
Swellin' round in Hart, Schaffner & Marx fancy suits,
And eatin' in rest'rants.
But somebody's got to stick to the old place,
Else Foxfield'd have to shut up shop,
Hey, Alice?"
"You admire him!
You admire Arthur!
You'd be like him only you can't dance.
Oh, Shame! Shame!
And I've been like that silly girl.
Fooled with your promises,
And I give you all I had.
I knew it, oh, I knew it,
But I wanted to git away 'fore I proved it.
You've shamed me through and through.
Why couldn't you hold your tongue,
And spared me seein' you
As you really are."
"What the Devil's the row?
I only said Art was lucky.
What you spitfirin' at me fer?
Ferget it, Alice.
We've had good times, ain't we?
I'll see Cleve 'bout that job agin to-morrer,

And we'll be married 'fore hayin' time."
"It's like you to remind me o' hayin' time.
I've good cause to love it, ain't I?
Many's the night I've hid my face in the dark
To shut out thinkin'!"
"Why, that ain't nothin'.
You ain't be'n half so kind to me
As lots o' fellers' girls.
Gi' me a kiss, Dear,
And let's make up."
"Make up!
You poor fool.
Do you suppose I care a ten cent piece
For you now.
You've killed yourself for me.
Done it out o' your own mouth.
You've took away my home,
I hate the sight o' the place.
You're all over it,
Every stick an' stone means you,
An' I hate 'em all."
"Alice, I say,
Don't go on like that.
I can't marry yer
Boardin' in one room,
But I'll see Cleve to-morrer,
I'll make him—"
"Oh, you fool!
You terrible fool!"
"Alice, don't go yit,
Wait a minit,
I'll see Cleve—"
"You terrible fool!"
"Alice, don't go.
Alice—" (Door slams)

AMY LOWELL

Number 3 on the Docket

The lawyer, are you?
Well! I ain't got nothin' to say.
Nothin'!
I told the perlice I hadn't nothin'.
They know'd real well 'twas me.
Ther warn't no supposin',
Ketchin' me in the woods as they did,
An' me in my house dress.
Folks don't walk miles an' miles
In the drifted snow,
With no hat nor wrap on 'em
Ef everythin's all right, I guess.
All right? Ha! Ha! Ha!
Nothin' warn't right with me.
Never was.
Oh, Lord! Why did I do it?
Why ain't it yesterday, and Ed here agin?
Many's the time I've set up with him nights
When he had cramps, or rheumatizm, or somethin'.
I used ter nurse him same's ef he was a baby.
I wouldn't hurt him, I love him!
Don't you dare to say I killed him. 'Twarn't me!
Somethin' got aholt o' me. I couldn't help it.
Oh, what shall I do! What shall I do!
Yes, Sir.
No, Sir.
I beg your pardon, I—I—
Oh, I'm a wicked woman!
An' I'm desolate, desolate!
Why warn't I struck dead or paralyzed
Afore my hands done it.
Oh, my God, what shall I do!
No, Sir, ther ain't no extenuatin' circumstances,
An' I don't want none.
I want a bolt o' lightnin'
To strike me dead right now!

Oh, I'll tell yer.
But it won't make no diff'rence.
Nothin' will.
Yes, I killed him.
Why do yer make me say it?
It's cruel! Cruel!
I killed him because o' th' silence.
The long, long silence,
That watched all around me,
And he wouldn't break it.
I tried to make him,
Time an' agin,
But he was terrible taciturn, Ed was.
He never spoke 'cept when he had to,
An' then he'd only say "yes" and "no."
You can't even guess what that silence was.
I'd hear it whisperin' in my ears,
An' I got frightened, 'twas so thick,
An' al'ays comin' back.
Ef Ed would ha' talked sometimes
It would ha' driven it away;
But he never would.
He didn't hear it same as I did.
You see, Sir,
Our farm was off'n the main road,
And set away back under the mountain;
And the village was seven mile off,
Measurin' after you'd got out o' our lane.
We didn't have no hired man,
'Cept in hayin' time;
An' Dane's place,
That was the nearest,
Was clear way 'tother side the mountain.
They used Marley post-office
An' ours was Benton.
Ther was a cart-track took yer to Dane's in Summer,
An' it warn't above two mile that way,
But it warn't never broke out Winters.
I used to dread the Winters.

Seem's ef I couldn't abear to see the golden-rod bloomin';
Winter'd come so quick after that.
You don't know what snow's like when yer with it
Day in an' day out.
Ed would be out all day loggin',
An' I set at home and look at the snow
Layin' over everythin';
It 'ud dazzle me blind,
Till it warn't white any more, but black as ink.
Then the quiet 'ud commence rushin' past my ears
Till I most went mad listenin' to it.
Many's the time I've dropped a pan on the floor
Jest to hear it clatter.
I was most frantic when dinner-time come
An' Ed was back from the woods.
I'd ha' give my soul to hear him speak.
But he'd never say a word till I asked him
Did he like the raised biscuits or whatever,
An' then sometimes he'd jest nod his answer.
Then he'd go out agin,
An' I'd watch him from the kitchin winder.
It seemed the woods come marchin' out to meet him
An' the trees 'ud press round him an' hustle him.
I got so I was scared o' th' trees.
I thought they come nearer,
Every day a little nearer,
Closin' up round the house.
I never went in t' th' woods Winters,
Though in Summer I liked 'em well enough.
It warn't so bad when my little boy was with us.
He used to go sleddin' and skatin',
An' every day his father fetched him to school in the pung
An' brought him back agin.
We scraped an' scraped fer Neddy,
We wanted him to have a education.
We sent him to High School,
An' then he went up to Boston to Technology.
He was a minin' engineer,
An' doin' real well,

A credit to his bringin' up.
But his very first position ther was an explosion in the mine.
And I'm glad! I'm glad!
He ain't here to see me now.
Neddy! Neddy!
I'm your mother still, Neddy.
Don't turn from me like that.
I can't abear it. I can't! I can't!
What did you say?
Oh, yes, Sir.
I'm here.
I'm very sorry,
I don't know what I'm sayin'.
No, Sir,
Not till after Neddy died.
'Twas the next Winter the silence come,
I don't remember noticin' it afore.
That was five year ago,
An' it's been gittin' worse an' worse.
I asked Ed to put in a telephone.
I thought ef I felt the whisperin' comin' on
I could ring up some o' th' folks.
But Ed wouldn't hear of it.
He said we'd paid so much for Neddy
We couldn't hardly git along as 'twas.
An' he never understood me wantin' to talk.
Well, this year was worse'n all the others;
We had a terrible spell o' stormy weather,
An' the snow lay so thick
You couldn't see the fences even.
Out o' doors was as flat as the palm o' my hand,
Ther warn't a hump or a holler
Fer as you could see.
It was so quiet
The snappin' o' the branches back in the wood-lot
Sounded like pistol shots.
Ed was out all day
Same as usual.
An' it seemed he talked less'n ever.

He didn't even say 'Good-mornin'', once or twice,
An' jest nodded or shook his head when I asked him things.
On Monday he said he'd got to go over to Benton
Fer some oats.
I'd oughter ha' gone with him,
But 'twas washin' day
An' I was afeared the fine weather'd break,
An' I couldn't do my dryin'.
All my life I'd done my work punctual,
An' I couldn't fix my conscience
To go junketin' on a washin'-day.
I can't tell you what that day was to me.
It dragged an' dragged,
Fer ther warn't no Ed ter break it in the middle
Fer dinner.
Every time I stopped stirrin' the water
I heerd the whisperin' all about me.
I stopped oftener'n I should
To see ef 'twas still ther,
An' it al'ays was.
An' gittin' louder
It seemed ter me.
Once I threw up the winder to feel the wind.
That seemed most alive somehow.
But the woods looked so kind of menacin'
I closed it quick
An' started to mangle's hard's I could,
The squeakin' was comfortin'.
Well, Ed come home 'bout four.
I seen him down the road,
An' I run out through the shed inter th' barn
To meet him quicker.
I hollered out, 'Hullo!'
But he didn't say nothin',
He jest drove right in
An' climbed out o' th' sleigh
An' commenced unharnessin'.
I asked him a heap o' questions;
Who he'd seed

An' what he'd done.
Once in a while he'd nod or shake,
But most o' th' time he didn't do nothin'.
'Twas gittin' dark then,
An' I was in a state,
With the loneliness
An' Ed payin' no attention
Like somethin' warn't livin'.
All of a sudden it come,
I don't know what,
But I jest couldn't stand no more.
It didn't seem 's though that was Ed,
An' it didn't seem as though I was me.
I had to break a way out somehow,
Somethin' was closin' in
An' I was stiflin'.
Ed's loggin' axe was ther,
An' I took it.
Oh, my God!
I can't see nothin' else afore me all the time.
I run out inter th' woods,
Seemed as ef they was pullin' me;
An' all the time I was wadin' through the snow
I seed Ed in front of me
Where I'd laid him.
An' I see him now.
There! There!
What you holdin' me fer?
I want ter go to Ed,
He's bleedin'.
Stop holdin' me.
I got to go.
I'm comin', Ed.
I'll be ther in a minit.
Oh, I'm so tired!
        (Faints)

CLOCKS TICK A CENTURY

Nightmare: A Tale for an Autumn Evening

After a Print by George Cruikshank

It was a gusty night,
With the wind booming, and swooping,
Looping round corners,
Sliding over the cobble-stones,
Whipping and veering,
And careering over the roofs
Like a thousand clattering horses.
Mr. Spruggins had been dining in the city,
Mr. Spruggins was none too steady in his gait,
And the wind played ball with Mr. Spruggins
And laughed as it whistled past him.
It rolled him along the street,
With his little feet pit-a-patting on the flags of the sidewalk,
And his muffler and his coat-tails blown straight out behind him.
It bumped him against area railings,
And chuckled in his ear when he said "Ouch!"
Sometimes it lifted him clear off his little patting feet
And bore him in triumph over three grey flagstones and a quarter.
The moon dodged in and out of clouds, winking.
It was all very unpleasant for Mr. Spruggins,
And when the wind flung him hard against his own front door
It was a relief,
Although the breath was quite knocked out of him.
The gas-lamp in front of the house flared up,
And the keyhole was as big as a barn door;
The gas-lamp flickered away to a sputtering blue star,
And the keyhole went out with it.
Such a stabbing, and jabbing,
And sticking, and picking,
And poking, and pushing, and prying
With that key;
And there is no denying that Mr. Spruggins rapped out an oath or two,
Rub-a-dub-dubbing them out to a real snare-drum roll.
But the door opened at last,

And Mr. Spruggins blew through it into his own hall
And slammed the door to so hard
That the knocker banged five times before it stopped.
Mr. Spruggins struck a light and lit a candle,
And all the time the moon winked at him through the window.
"Why couldn't you find the keyhole, Spruggins?"
Taunted the wind.
"I can find the keyhole."
And the wind, thin as a wire,
Darted in and seized the candle flame
And knocked it over to one side
And pummelled it down—down—down—!
But Mr. Spruggins held the candle so close that it singed his chin,
And ran and stumbled up the stairs in a surprisingly agile manner,
For the wind through the keyhole kept saying, "Spruggins! Spruggins!"
    behind him.
The fire in his bedroom burned brightly.
The room with its crimson bed and window curtains
Was as red and glowing as a carbuncle.
It was still and warm.
There was no wind here, for the windows were fastened;
And no moon,
For the curtains were drawn.
The candle flame stood up like a pointed pear
In a wide brass dish.
Mr. Spruggins sighed with content;
He was safe at home.
The fire glowed—red and yellow roses
In the black basket of the grate—
And the bed with its crimson hangings
Seemed a great peony,
Wide open and placid.
Mr. Spruggins slipped off his top-coat and his muffler.
He slipped off his bottle-green coat
And his flowered waistcoat.
He put on a flannel dressing-gown,
And tied a peaked night-cap under his chin.
He wound his large gold watch
And placed it under his pillow.

Then he tiptoed over to the window and pulled back the curtain.
There was the moon dodging in and out of the clouds;
But behind him was his quiet candle.
There was the wind whisking along the street.
The window rattled, but it was fastened.
Did the wind say, "Spruggins"?
All Mr. Spruggins heard was "S-s-s-s-s—"
Dying away down the street.
He dropped the curtain and got into bed.
Martha had been in the last thing with the warming-pan;
The bed was warm,
And Mr. Spruggins sank into feathers,
With the familiar ticking of his watch just under his head.
Mr. Spruggins dozed.
He had forgotten to put out the candle,
But it did not make much difference as the fire was so bright. . .
Too bright!
The red and yellow roses pricked his eyelids,
They scorched him back to consciousness.
He tried to shift his position;
He could not move.
Something weighed him down,
He could not breathe.
He was gasping,
Pinned down and suffocating.
He opened his eyes.
The curtains of the window were flung back,
The fire and the candle were out,
And the room was filled with green moonlight.
And pressed against the window-pane
Was a wide, round face,
Winking—winking—
Solemnly dropping one eyelid after the other.
Tick—tock—went the watch under his pillow,
Wink—wink—went the face at the window.
It was not the fire roses which had pricked him,
It was the winking eyes.
Mr. Spruggins tried to bounce up;
He could not, because—

His heart flapped up into his mouth
And fell back dead.
On his chest was a fat pink pig,
On the pig a blackamoor
With a ten pound weight for a cap.
His mustachios kept curling up and down like angry snakes,
And his eyes rolled round and round,
With the pupils coming into sight, and disappearing,
And appearing again on the other side.
The holsters at his saddle-bow were two port bottles,
And a curved table-knife hung at his belt for a scimitar,
While a fork and a keg of spirits were strapped to the saddle behind.
He dug his spurs into the pig,
Which trampled and snorted,
And stamped its cloven feet deeper into Mr. Spruggins.
Then the green light on the floor began to undulate.
It heaved and hollowed,
It rose like a tide,
Sea-green,
Full of claws and scales
And wriggles.
The air above his bed began to move;
It weighed over him
In a mass of draggled feathers.
Not one lifted to stir the air.
They drooped and dripped
With a smell of port wine and brandy,
Closing down, slowly,
Trickling drops on the bed-quilt.
Suddenly the window fell in with a great scatter of glass,
And the moon burst into the room,
Sizzling—"S-s-s-s-s—Spruggins! Spruggins!"
It rolled toward him,
A green ball of flame,
With two eyes in the center,
A red eye and a yellow eye,
Dropping their lids slowly,
One after the other.
Mr. Spruggins tried to scream,

But the blackamoor
Leapt off his pig
With a cry,
Drew his scimitar,
And plunged it into Mr. Spruggins's mouth.

Mr. Spruggins got up in the cold dawn
And remade the fire.
Then he crept back to bed
By the light which seeped in under the window curtains,
And lay there, shivering,
While the bells of St. George the Martyr chimed the quarter after
    seven.

The Paper Windmill

The little boy pressed his face against the window-pane and looked out at the bright sunshiny morning. The cobble-stones of the square glistened like mica. In the trees, a breeze danced and pranced, and shook drops of sunlight like falling golden coins into the brown water of the canal. Down stream slowly drifted a long string of galliots piled with crimson cheeses. The little boy thought they looked as if they were roc's eggs, blocks of big ruby eggs. He said, "Oh!" with delight, and pressed against the window with all his might.

The golden cock on the top of the 'Stadhuis' gleamed. His beak was open like a pair of scissors and a narrow piece of blue sky was wedged in it. "Cock-a-doodle-do," cried the little boy. "Can't you hear me through the window, Gold Cocky? Cock-a-doodle-do! You should crow when you see the eggs of your cousin, the great roc." But the golden cock stood stock still, with his fine tail blowing in the wind. He could not understand the little boy, for he said "Cocorico" when he said anything. But he was hung in the air to swing, not to sing. His eyes glittered to the bright West wind, and the crimson cheeses drifted away down the canal.

It was very dull there in the big room. Outside in the square, the wind was playing tag with some fallen leaves. A man passed, with a dogcart beside him full of smart, new milkcans. They rattled out a gay tune: "Tiddity-tum-ti-ti. Have some milk for your tea. Cream for your coffee to drink tonight, thick, and smooth, and sweet, and white," and the man's sabots beat an accompaniment: "Plop! trop! milk for your tea. Plop! trop! drink it tonight." It was very pleasant out there, but it was lonely here in the big room. The little boy gulped at a tear.

It was queer how dull all his toys were. They were so still. Nothing was still in the square. If he took his eyes away a moment it had changed. The milkman had disappeared round the corner, there was only an old woman with a basket of green stuff on her head, picking her way over the shiny stones. But the wind pulled the leaves in the basket this way and that, and displayed them to beautiful advantage. The sun patted them condescendingly on their flat surfaces, and they seemed sprinkled with silver. The little boy sighed as he looked at his disordered toys on the floor. They were motionless, and their colours were dull. The dark wainscoting absorbed the sun. There was none left for toys.

The square was quite empty now. Only the wind ran round and round it, spinning. Away over in the corner where a street opened into the square, the wind had stopped. Stopped running, that is, for it never stopped spinning. It whirred, and whirled, and gyrated, and turned. It burned like a great coloured sun. It hummed, and buzzed, and sparked, and darted. There were flashes of blue, and long smearing lines of saffron, and quick jabs of green. And over it all was a sheen like a myriad cut diamonds. Round and round it went, the huge wind-wheel, and the little boy's head reeled with watching it. The whole square was filled with its rays, blazing and leaping round after one another, faster and faster. The little boy could not speak, he could only gaze, staring in amaze.

The wind-wheel was coming down the square. Nearer and nearer it came, a great disk of spinning flame. It was opposite the window now, and the little boy could see it plainly, but it was something more than the wind which he saw. A man was carrying a huge fan-shaped frame on his shoulder, and stuck in it were many little painted paper windmills, each one scurrying round in the breeze. They were bright and beautiful, and the sight was one to please anybody, and how much more a little boy who had only stupid, motionless toys to enjoy.

The little boy clapped his hands, and his eyes danced and whizzed, for the circling windmills made him dizzy. Closer and closer came the windmill man, and held up his big fan to the little boy in the window of the Ambassador's house. Only a pane of glass between the boy and the windmills. They slid round before his eyes in rapidly revolving splendour. There were wheels and wheels of colours—big, little, thick, thin—all one clear, perfect spin. The windmill vendor dipped and raised them again, and the little boy's face was glued to the window-pane. Oh! What a glorious, wonderful plaything! Rings and rings of windy colour always moving! How had any one ever preferred those other toys which never stirred. "Nursie, come quickly. Look! I want a windmill. See! It is never still. You will buy me one, won't you? I want that silver one, with the big ring of blue."

So a servant was sent to buy that one: silver, ringed with blue, and smartly it twirled about in the servant's hands as he stood a moment to pay the vendor. Then he entered the house, and in another minute he was standing in the nursery door, with some crumpled paper on the end of a stick which he held out to the little boy. "But I wanted a windmill which went round," cried the little boy. "That is the one you asked for, Master Charles," Nursie was a bit impatient, she had mending to do. "See, it is silver, and here is the blue." "But it is only a blue streak," sobbed the little boy. "I wanted a blue ring, and this silver doesn't sparkle." "Well, Master Charles, that is what you wanted, now run away and play with it, for I am very busy."

The little boy hid his tears against the friendly window-pane. On the floor lay the motionless, crumpled bit of paper on the end of its stick. But far away across the square was the windmill vendor, with his big wheel of whirring splendour. It spun round in a blaze like a whirling rainbow, and the sun gleamed upon it, and the wind whipped it, until it seemed a maze of spattering diamonds. "Cocorico!" crowed the golden cock on the top of the 'Stadhuis'. "That is something worth crowing for." But the little boy did not hear him, he was sobbing over the crumpled bit of paper on the floor.

The Red Lacquer Music-Stand

A music-stand of crimson lacquer, long since brought
In some fast clipper-ship from China, quaintly wrought
With bossed and carven flowers and fruits in blackening gold,
The slender shaft all twined about and thickly scrolled
With vine leaves and young twisted tendrils, whirling, curling,
Flinging their new shoots over the four wings, and swirling
Out on the three wide feet in golden lumps and streams;
Petals and apples in high relief, and where the seams
Are worn with handling, through the polished crimson sheen,
Long streaks of black, the under lacquer, shine out clean.
Four desks, adjustable, to suit the heights of players
Sitting to viols or standing up to sing, four layers
Of music to serve every instrument, are there,
And on the apex a large flat-topped golden pear.
It burns in red and yellow, dusty, smouldering lights,
When the sun flares the old barn-chamber with its flights
And skips upon the crystal knobs of dim sideboards,
Legless and mouldy, and hops, glint to glint, on hoards
Of scythes, and spades, and dinner-horns, so the old tools
Are little candles throwing brightness round in pools.
With Oriental splendour, red and gold, the dust
Covering its flames like smoke and thinning as a gust
Of brighter sunshine makes the colours leap and range,
The strange old music-stand seems to strike out and change;
To stroke and tear the darkness with sharp golden claws;
To dart a forked, vermilion tongue from open jaws;
To puff out bitter smoke which chokes the sun; and fade
Back to a still, faint outline obliterate in shade.
Creeping up the ladder into the loft, the Boy
Stands watching, very still, prickly and hot with joy.
He sees the dusty sun-mote slit by streaks of red,
He sees it split and stream, and all about his head
Spikes and spears of gold are licking, pricking, flicking,
Scratching against the walls and furniture, and nicking
The darkness into sparks, chipping away the gloom.
The Boy's nose smarts with the pungence in the room.

The wind pushes an elm branch from before the door
And the sun widens out all along the floor,
Filling the barn-chamber with white, straightforward light,
So not one blurred outline can tease the mind to fright.

> "O All ye Works of the Lord, Bless ye the Lord; Praise Him, and
>   Magnify Him for ever.
> O let the Earth Bless the Lord; Yea, let it Praise Him, and
>   Magnify Him for ever.
> O ye Mountains and Hills, Bless ye the Lord; Praise Him, and
>   Magnify Him for ever.
> O All ye Green Things upon the Earth, Bless ye the Lord; Praise
>   Him, and Magnify Him for ever."

The Boy will praise his God on an altar builded fair,
Will heap it with the Works of the Lord. In the morning air,
Spices shall burn on it, and by their pale smoke curled,
Like shoots of all the Green Things, the God of this bright World
Shall see the Boy's desire to pay his debt of praise.
The Boy turns round about, seeking with careful gaze
An altar meet and worthy, but each table and chair
Has some defect, each piece is needing some repair
To perfect it; the chairs have broken legs and backs,
The tables are uneven, and every highboy lacks
A handle or a drawer, the desks are bruised and worn,
And even a wide sofa has its cane seat torn.
Only in the gloom far in the corner there
The lacquer music-stand is elegant and rare,
Clear and slim of line, with its four wings outspread,
The sound of old quartets, a tenuous, faint thread,
Hanging and floating over it, it stands supreme—
Black, and gold, and crimson, in one twisted scheme!

A candle on the bookcase feels a draught and wavers,
Stippling the white-washed walls with dancing shades and quavers.
A bed-post, grown colossal, jigs about the ceiling,
And shadows, strangely altered, stain the walls, revealing
Eagles, and rabbits, and weird faces pulled awry,
And hands which fetch and carry things incessantly.

Under the Eastern window, where the morning sun
Must touch it, stands the music-stand, and on each one
Of its broad platforms is a pyramid of stones,
And metals, and dried flowers, and pine and hemlock cones,
An oriole's nest with the four eggs neatly blown,
The rattle of a rattlesnake, and three large brown
Butternuts uncracked, six butterflies impaled
With a green luna moth, a snake-skin freshly scaled,
Some sunflower seeds, wampum, and a bloody-tooth shell,
A blue jay feather, all together piled pell-mell
The stand will hold no more. The Boy with humming head
Looks once again, blows out the light, and creeps to bed.

The Boy keeps solemn vigil, while outside the wind
Blows gustily and clear, and slaps against the blind.
He hardly tries to sleep, so sharp his ecstasy
It burns his soul to emptiness, and sets it free
For adoration only, for worship. Dedicate,
His unsheathed soul is naked in its novitiate.
The hours strike below from the clock on the stair.
The Boy is a white flame suspiring in prayer.
Morning will bring the sun, the Golden Eye of Him
Whose splendour must be veiled by starry cherubim,
Whose Feet shimmer like crystal in the streets of Heaven.
Like an open rose the sun will stand up even,
Fronting the window-sill, and when the casement glows
Rose-red with the new-blown morning, then the fire which flows
From the sun will fall upon the altar and ignite
The spices, and his sacrifice will burn in perfumed light.
Over the music-stand the ghosts of sounds will swim,
'Viols d'amore' and 'hautbois' accorded to a hymn.
The Boy will see the faintest breath of angels' wings
Fanning the smoke, and voices will flower through the strings.
He dares no farther vision, and with scalding eyes
Waits upon the daylight and his great emprise.

The cold, grey light of dawn was whitening the wall
When the Boy, fine-drawn by sleeplessness, started his ritual.
He washed, all shivering and pointed like a flame.

He threw the shutters open, and in the window-frame
The morning glimmered like a tarnished Venice glass.
He took his Chinese pastilles and put them in a mass
Upon the mantelpiece till he could seek a plate
Worthy to hold them burning. Alas! He had been late
In thinking of this need, and now he could not find
Platter or saucer rare enough to ease his mind.
The house was not astir, and he dared not go down
Into the barn-chamber, lest some door should be blown
And slam before the draught he made as he went out.
The light was growing yellower, and still he looked about.
A flash of almost crimson from the gilded pear
Upon the music-stand, startled him waiting there.
The sun would rise and he would meet it unprepared,
Labelled a fool in having missed what he had dared.
He ran across the room, took his pastilles and laid
Them on the flat-topped pear, most carefully displayed
To light with ease, then stood a little to one side,
Focussed a burning-glass and painstakingly tried
To hold it angled so the bunched and prismed rays
Should leap upon each other and spring into a blaze.
Sharp as a wheeling edge of disked, carnation flame,
Gem-hard and cutting upward, slowly the round sun came.
The arrowed fire caught the burning-glass and glanced,
Split to a multitude of pointed spears, and lanced,
A deeper, hotter flame, it took the incense pile
Which welcomed it and broke into a little smile
Of yellow flamelets, creeping, crackling, thrusting up,
A golden, red-slashed lily in a lacquer cup.

"O ye Fire and Heat, Bless ye the Lord; Praise Him, and Magnify
Him for ever.
O ye Winter and Summer, Bless ye the Lord; Praise Him, and
Magnify Him for ever.
O ye Nights and Days, Bless ye the Lord; Praise Him, and
Magnify Him for ever.
O ye Lightnings and Clouds, Bless ye the Lord; Praise Him, and
Magnify Him for ever."

A moment so it hung, wide-curved, bright-petalled, seeming
A chalice foamed with sunrise. The Boy woke from his dreaming.
A spike of flame had caught the card of butterflies,
The oriole's nest took fire, soon all four galleries
Where he had spread his treasures were become one tongue
Of gleaming, brutal fire. The Boy instantly swung
His pitcher off the wash-stand and turned it upside down.
The flames drooped back and sizzled, and all his senses grown
Acute by fear, the Boy grabbed the quilt from his bed
And flung it over all, and then with aching head
He watched the early sunshine glint on the remains
Of his holy offering. The lacquer stand had stains
Ugly and charred all over, and where the golden pear
Had been, a deep, black hole gaped miserably. His dear
Treasures were puffs of ashes; only the stones were there,
Winking in the brightness.
                                    The clock upon the stair
Struck five, and in the kitchen someone shook a grate.
The Boy began to dress, for it was getting late.

Spring Day

Bath

THE DAY IS FRESH-WASHED AND fair, and there is a smell of tulips and narcissus in the air.

The sunshine pours in at the bath-room window and bores through the water in the bath-tub in lathes and planes of greenish-white. It cleaves the water into flaws like a jewel, and cracks it to bright light.

Little spots of sunshine lie on the surface of the water and dance, dance, and their reflections wobble deliciously over the ceiling; a stir of my finger sets them whirring, reeling. I move a foot, and the planes of light in the water jar. I lie back and laugh, and let the green-white water, the sun-flawed beryl water, flow over me. The day is almost too bright to bear, the green water covers me from the too bright day. I will lie here awhile and play with the water and the sun spots.

The sky is blue and high. A crow flaps by the window, and there is a whiff of tulips and narcissus in the air.

Breakfast Table

IN THE FRESH-WASHED SUNLIGHT, THE breakfast table is decked and white. It offers itself in flat surrender, tendering tastes, and smells, and colours, and metals, and grains, and the white cloth falls over its side, draped and wide. Wheels of white glitter in the silver coffee-pot, hot and spinning like catherine-wheels, they whirl, and twirl—and my eyes begin to smart, the little white, dazzling wheels prick them like darts. Placid and peaceful, the rolls of bread spread themselves in the sun to bask. A stack of butter-pats, pyramidal, shout orange through the white, scream, flutter, call: "Yellow! Yellow! Yellow!" Coffee steam rises in a stream, clouds the silver tea-service with mist, and twists up into the sunlight, revolved, involuted, suspiring higher and higher, fluting in a thin spiral up the high blue sky. A crow flies by and croaks at the coffee steam. The day is new and fair with good smells in the air.

Walk

OVER THE STREET THE WHITE clouds meet, and sheer away without touching.

On the sidewalks, boys are playing marbles. Glass marbles, with amber and blue hearts, roll together and part with a sweet clashing noise. The boys strike them with black and red striped agates. The glass marbles spit crimson when they are hit, and slip into the gutters under rushing brown water. I smell tulips and narcissus in the air, but there are no flowers anywhere, only white dust whipping up the street, and a girl with a gay Spring hat and blowing skirts. The dust and the wind flirt at her ankles and her neat, high-heeled patent leather shoes. Tap, tap, the little heels pat the pavement, and the wind rustles among the flowers on her hat.

A water-cart crawls slowly on the other side of the way. It is green and gay with new paint, and rumbles contentedly, sprinkling clear water over the white dust. Clear zigzagging water, which smells of tulips and narcissus.

The thickening branches make a pink 'grisaille' against the blue sky.

Whoop! The clouds go dashing at each other and sheer away just in time. Whoop! And a man's hat careers down the street in front of the white dust, leaps into the branches of a tree, veers away and trundles ahead of the wind, jarring the sunlight into spokes of rose-colour and green.

A motor-car cuts a swathe through the bright air, sharp-beaked, irresistible, shouting to the wind to make way. A glare of dust and sunshine tosses together behind it, and settles down. The sky is quiet and high, and the morning is fair with fresh-washed air.

Midday and Afternoon

SWIRL OF CROWDED STREETS. SHOCK and recoil of traffic. The stock-still brick facade of an old church, against which the waves of people lurch and withdraw. Flare of sunshine down side-streets. Eddies of light in the windows of chemists' shops, with their blue, gold, purple jars, darting colours far into the crowd. Loud bangs and tremors, murmurings out of high windows, whirring of machine belts, blurring of horses and motors. A quick spin and shudder of brakes on an electric car, and the jar of a church-bell knocking against the metal blue of the sky. I am a piece of the town, a bit of blown dust, thrust along with the crowd. Proud to feel the pavement under me, reeling with feet. Feet tripping, skipping, lagging, dragging, plodding doggedly, or springing up and advancing on firm elastic insteps. A boy is selling papers, I smell them clean and new from the press. They are fresh like the air, and pungent as tulips and narcissus.

The blue sky pales to lemon, and great tongues of gold blind the shop-windows, putting out their contents in a flood of flame.

Night and Sleep

THE DAY TAKES HER EASE in slippered yellow. Electric signs gleam out along the shop fronts, following each other. They grow, and grow, and blow into patterns of fire-flowers as the sky fades. Trades scream in spots of light at the unruffled night. Twinkle, jab, snap, that means a new play; and over the way: plop, drop, quiver, is the sidelong sliver of a watchmaker's sign with its length on another street. A gigantic mug of beer effervesces to the atmosphere over a tall building, but the sky is high and has her own stars, why should she heed ours?

I leave the city with speed. Wheels whirl to take me back to my trees and my quietness. The breeze which blows with me is fresh-washed and clean, it has come but recently from the high sky. There are no flowers in bloom yet, but the earth of my garden smells of tulips and narcissus.

My room is tranquil and friendly. Out of the window I can see the distant city, a band of twinkling gems, little flower-heads with no stems. I cannot see the beer-glass, nor the letters of the restaurants and shops I passed, now the signs blur and all together make the city, glowing on a night of fine weather, like a garden stirring and blowing for the Spring.

The night is fresh-washed and fair and there is a whiff of flowers in the air.

Wrap me close, sheets of lavender. Pour your blue and purple dreams into my ears. The breeze whispers at the shutters and mutters queer tales of old days, and cobbled streets, and youths leaping their horses down marble stairways. Pale blue lavender, you are the colour of the sky when it is fresh-washed and fair. . . I smell the stars. . . they are like tulips and narcissus. . . I smell them in the air.

The Dinner-Party

Fish

"So. . ." they said,
With their wine-glasses delicately poised,
Mocking at the thing they cannot understand.
"So. . ." they said again,
Amused and insolent.
The silver on the table glittered,
And the red wine in the glasses
Seemed the blood I had wasted
In a foolish cause.

Game

The gentleman with the grey-and-black whiskers
Sneered languidly over his quail.
Then my heart flew up and laboured,
And I burst from my own holding
And hurled myself forward.
With straight blows I beat upon him,
Furiously, with red-hot anger, I thrust against him.
But my weapon slithered over his polished surface,
And I recoiled upon myself,
Panting.

Drawing-Room

In a dress all softness and half-tones,
Indolent and half-reclined,
She lay upon a couch,
With the firelight reflected in her jewels.
But her eyes had no reflection,
They swam in a grey smoke,
The smoke of smouldering ashes,
The smoke of her cindered heart.

Coffee

They sat in a circle with their coffee-cups.
One dropped in a lump of sugar,
One stirred with a spoon.
I saw them as a circle of ghosts
Sipping blackness out of beautiful china,
And mildly protesting against my coarseness
In being alive.

Talk

They took dead men's souls
And pinned them on their breasts for ornament;
Their cuff-links and tiaras
Were gems dug from a grave;
They were ghouls battening on exhumed thoughts;
And I took a green liqueur from a servant
So that he might come near me
And give me the comfort of a living thing.

Eleven O'Clock

The front door was hard and heavy,
It shut behind me on the house of ghosts.
I flattened my feet on the pavement
To feel it solid under me;
I ran my hand along the railings
And shook them,
And pressed their pointed bars
Into my palms.
The hurt of it reassured me,
And I did it again and again
Until they were bruised.
When I woke in the night
I laughed to find them aching,
For only living flesh can suffer.

Stravinsky's Three Pieces "Grotesques," for String Quartet

First Movement

Thin-voiced, nasal pipes
Drawing sound out and out
Until it is a screeching thread,
Sharp and cutting, sharp and cutting,
It hurts.
Whee-e-e!
Bump! Bump! Tong-ti-bump!
There are drums here,
Banging,
And wooden shoes beating the round, grey stones
Of the market-place.
Whee-e-e!
Sabots slapping the worn, old stones,
And a shaking and cracking of dancing bones;
Clumsy and hard they are,
And uneven,
Losing half a beat
Because the stones are slippery.
Bump-e-ty-tong! Whee-e-e! Tong!
The thin Spring leaves
Shake to the banging of shoes.
Shoes beat, slap,
Shuffle, rap,
And the nasal pipes squeal with their pigs' voices,
Little pigs' voices
Weaving among the dancers,
A fine white thread
Linking up the dancers.
Bang! Bump! Tong!
Petticoats,
Stockings,
Sabots,
Delirium flapping its thigh-bones;

Red, blue, yellow,
Drunkenness steaming in colours;
Red, yellow, blue,
Colours and flesh weaving together,
In and out, with the dance,
Coarse stuffs and hot flesh weaving together.
Pigs' cries white and tenuous,
White and painful,
White and—
Bump!
Tong!

Second Movement

Pale violin music whiffs across the moon,
A pale smoke of violin music blows over the moon,
Cherry petals fall and flutter,
And the white Pierrot,
Wreathed in the smoke of the violins,
Splashed with cherry petals falling, falling,
Claws a grave for himself in the fresh earth
With his finger-nails.

Third Movement

An organ growls in the heavy roof-groins of a church,
It wheezes and coughs.
The nave is blue with incense,
Writhing, twisting,
Snaking over the heads of the chanting priests.
    'Requiem aeternam dona ei, Domine';
The priests whine their bastard Latin
And the censers swing and click.
The priests walk endlessly
Round and round,
Droning their Latin
Off the key.
The organ crashes out in a flaring chord,
And the priests hitch their chant up half a tone.

    'Dies illa, dies irae,
    Calamitatis et miseriae,
    Dies magna et amara valde.'
A wind rattles the leaded windows.
The little pear-shaped candle flames leap and flutter,
    'Dies illa, dies irae;'
The swaying smoke drifts over the altar,
    'Calamitatis et miseriae;'
The shuffling priests sprinkle holy water,
    'Dies magna et amara valde;'
And there is a stark stillness in the midst of them
Stretched upon a bier.
His ears are stone to the organ,
His eyes are flint to the candles,
His body is ice to the water.
Chant, priests,
Whine, shuffle, genuflect,
He will always be as rigid as he is now
Until he crumbles away in a dust heap.
    'Lacrymosa dies illa,
    Qua resurget ex favilla
    Judicandus homo reus.'
Above the grey pillars the roof is in darkness.

Towns in Colour

I

Red Slippers

RED SLIPPERS IN A SHOP-WINDOW, and outside in the street, flaws of grey, windy sleet!

Behind the polished glass, the slippers hang in long threads of red, festooning from the ceiling like stalactites of blood, flooding the eyes of passers-by with dripping colour, jamming their crimson reflections against the windows of cabs and tram-cars, screaming their claret and salmon into the teeth of the sleet, plopping their little round maroon lights upon the tops of umbrellas.

The row of white, sparkling shop fronts is gashed and bleeding, it bleeds red slippers. They spout under the electric light, fluid and fluctuating, a hot rain—and freeze again to red slippers, myriadly multiplied in the mirror side of the window.

They balance upon arched insteps like springing bridges of crimson lacquer; they swing up over curved heels like whirling tanagers sucked in a wind-pocket; they flatten out, heelless, like July ponds, flared and burnished by red rockets.

Snap, snap, they are cracker-sparks of scarlet in the white, monotonous block of shops.

They plunge the clangour of billions of vermilion trumpets into the crowd outside, and echo in faint rose over the pavement.

People hurry by, for these are only shoes, and in a window, farther down, is a big lotus bud of cardboard whose petals open every few minutes and reveal a wax doll, with staring bead eyes and flaxen hair, lolling awkwardly in its flower chair.

One has often seen shoes, but whoever saw a cardboard lotus bud before?

The flaws of grey, windy sleet beat on the shop-window where there are only red slippers.

II

Thompson's Lunch Room—Grand Central Station

Study in Whites

Wax-white—
Floor, ceiling, walls.
Ivory shadows
Over the pavement
Polished to cream surfaces
By constant sweeping.
The big room is coloured like the petals
Of a great magnolia,
And has a patina
Of flower bloom
Which makes it shine dimly
Under the electric lamps.
Chairs are ranged in rows
Like sepia seeds
Waiting fulfilment.
The chalk-white spot of a cook's cap
Moves unglossily against the vaguely bright wall—
Dull chalk-white striking the retina like a blow
Through the wavering uncertainty of steam.
Vitreous-white of glasses with green reflections,
Ice-green carboys, shifting—greener, bluer—with the jar of moving
    water.
Jagged green-white bowls of pressed glass
Rearing snow-peaks of chipped sugar
Above the lighthouse-shaped castors
Of grey pepper and grey-white salt.
Grey-white placards: "Oyster Stew, Cornbeef Hash, Frankfurters":
Marble slabs veined with words in meandering lines.
Dropping on the white counter like horn notes
Through a web of violins,
The flat yellow lights of oranges,
The cube-red splashes of apples,
In high plated 'epergnes'.

The electric clock jerks every half-minute:
"Coming!—Past!"
"Three beef-steaks and a chicken-pie,"
Bawled through a slide while the clock jerks heavily.
A man carries a china mug of coffee to a distant chair.
Two rice puddings and a salmon salad
Are pushed over the counter;
The unfulfilled chairs open to receive them.
A spoon falls upon the floor with the impact of metal striking stone,
And the sound throws across the room
Sharp, invisible zigzags
Of silver.

III

An Opera House

Within the gold square of the proscenium arch,
A curtain of orange velvet hangs in stiff folds,
Its tassels jarring slightly when someone crosses the stage behind.
Gold carving edges the balconies,
Rims the boxes,
Runs up and down fluted pillars.
Little knife-stabs of gold
Shine out whenever a box door is opened.
Gold clusters
Flash in soft explosions
On the blue darkness,
Suck back to a point,
And disappear.
Hoops of gold
Circle necks, wrists, fingers,
Pierce ears,
Poise on heads
And fly up above them in coloured sparkles.
Gold!
Gold!
The opera house is a treasure-box of gold.
Gold in a broad smear across the orchestra pit:

Gold of horns, trumpets, tubas;
Gold—spun-gold, twittering-gold, snapping-gold
Of harps.
The conductor raises his baton,
The brass blares out
Crass, crude,
Parvenu, fat, powerful,
Golden.
Rich as the fat, clapping hands in the boxes.
Cymbals, gigantic, coin-shaped,
Crash.
The orange curtain parts
And the prima-donna steps forward.
One note,
A drop: transparent, iridescent,
A gold bubble,
It floats. . . floats. . .
And bursts against the lips of a bank president
In the grand tier.

IV

Afternoon Rain in State Street

Cross-hatchings of rain against grey walls,
Slant lines of black rain
In front of the up and down, wet stone sides of buildings.
Below,
Greasy, shiny, black, horizontal,
The street.
And over it, umbrellas,
Black polished dots
Struck to white
An instant,
Stream in two flat lines
Slipping past each other with the smoothness of oil.
Like a four-sided wedge
The Custom House Tower
Pokes at the low, flat sky,

Pushing it farther and farther up,
Lifting it away from the house-tops,
Lifting it in one piece as though it were a sheet of tin,
With the lever of its apex.
The cross-hatchings of rain cut the Tower obliquely,
Scratching lines of black wire across it,
Mutilating its perpendicular grey surface
With the sharp precision of tools.
The city is rigid with straight lines and angles,
A chequered table of blacks and greys.
Oblong blocks of flatness
Crawl by with low-geared engines,
And pass to short upright squares
Shrinking with distance.
A steamer in the basin blows its whistle,
And the sound shoots across the rain hatchings,
A narrow, level bar of steel.
Hard cubes of lemon
Superimpose themselves upon the fronts of buildings
As the windows light up.
But the lemon cubes are edged with angles
Upon which they cannot impinge.
Up, straight, down, straight—square.
Crumpled grey-white papers
Blow along the side-walks,
Contorted, horrible,
Without curves.
A horse steps in a puddle,
And white, glaring water spurts up
In stiff, outflaring lines,
Like the rattling stems of reeds.
The city is heraldic with angles,
A sombre escutcheon of argent and sable
And countercoloured bends of rain
Hung over a four-square civilization.
When a street lamp comes out,
I gaze at it for fully thirty seconds
To rest my brain with the suffusing, round brilliance of its
    globe.

V

An Aquarium

Streaks of green and yellow iridescence,
Silver shiftings,
Rings veering out of rings,
Silver—gold—
Grey-green opaqueness sliding down,
With sharp white bubbles
Shooting and dancing,
Flinging quickly outward.
Nosing the bubbles,
Swallowing them,
Fish.
Blue shadows against silver-saffron water,
The light rippling over them
In steel-bright tremors.
Outspread translucent fins
Flute, fold, and relapse;
The threaded light prints through them on the pebbles
In scarcely tarnished twinklings.
Curving of spotted spines,
Slow up-shifts,
Lazy convolutions:
Then a sudden swift straightening
And darting below:
Oblique grey shadows
Athwart a pale casement.
Roped and curled,
Green man-eating eels
Slumber in undulate rhythms,
With crests laid horizontal on their backs.
Barred fish,
Striped fish,
Uneven disks of fish,
Slip, slide, whirl, turn,
And never touch.
Metallic blue fish,

With fins wide and yellow and swaying
Like Oriental fans,
Hold the sun in their bellies
And glow with light:
Blue brilliance cut by black bars.
An oblong pane of straw-coloured shimmer,
Across it, in a tangent,
A smear of rose, black, silver.
Short twists and upstartings,
Rose-black, in a setting of bubbles:
Sunshine playing between red and black flowers
On a blue and gold lawn.
Shadows and polished surfaces,
Facets of mauve and purple,
A constant modulation of values.
Shaft-shaped,
With green bead eyes;
Thick-nosed,
Heliotrope-coloured;
Swift spots of chrysolite and coral;
In the midst of green, pearl, amethyst irradiations.

Outside,
A willow-tree flickers
With little white jerks,
And long blue waves
Rise steadily beyond the outer islands.

A Note About the Author

Amy Lowell (1874–1925) was an American poet. Born into an elite family of businessmen, politicians, and intellectuals, Lowell was a member of the so-called Boston Brahmin class. She excelled in school from a young age and developed a habit for reading and book collecting. Denied the opportunity to attend college by her family, Lowell traveled extensively in her twenties and turned to poetry in 1902. While in England with her lover Ada Dwyer Russell, she met American poet Ezra Pound, whose influence as an imagist and fierce critic of Lowell's work would prove essential to her poetry. In 1912, only two years after publishing her first poem in *The Atlantic Monthly*, Lowell produced *A Dome of Many-Coloured Glass,* her debut volume of poems. In addition to such collections of her own poems as *Sword Blades and Poppy Seed* (1914) and *Men, Women, and Ghosts* (1916), Lowell published translations of 8th century Chinese poet Li Tai-po and, at the time of her death, had been working on a biography of English Romantic John Keats.

A Note from the Publisher

Spanning many genres, from non-fiction essays to literature classics to children's books and lyric poetry, Mint Edition books showcase the master works of our time in a modern new package. The text is freshly typeset, is clean and easy to read, and features a new note about the author in each volume. Many books also include exclusive new introductory material. Every book boasts a striking new cover, which makes it as appropriate for collecting as it is for gift giving. Mint Edition books are only printed when a reader orders them, so natural resources are not wasted. We're proud that our books are never manufactured in excess and exist only in the exact quantity they need to be read and enjoyed.

Discover more of your favorite classics with Bookfinity™.

- Track your reading with custom book lists.
- Get great book recommendations for your personalized Reader Type.
- Add reviews for your favorite books.
- AND MUCH MORE!

Visit **bookfinity.com** and take the fun Reader Type quiz to get started.

Enjoy our classic and modern companion pairings!

Printed in the USA
CPSIA information can be obtained
at www.ICGtesting.com
JSHW022342140824
68134JS00019B/1639

9 781513 295879